GENESIS

The Book
of Origins

GENESIS

THE BOOK
OF ORIGINS

By

Rev. Albert Joseph Mary Shamon

Published by:
The Riehle Foundation
P.O. Box 7
Milford, OH 45150-0007 USA
513-576-0032

Nihil obstat: Reverend Robert J. Buschmiller
            August 27, 1997

Imprimatur: Most Reverend Carl K. Moeddel
            Vicar General and Auxiliary Bishop
            Cincinnati, Ohio
            September 15, 1997

The *Nihil obstat* and the *Imprimatur* are a declaration that a book or pamphlet is considered to be free from doctrinal or moral error. It is not implied that those who have granted the Nihil obstat and Imprimatur agree with the contents, opinions or statements expressed.

Published by The Riehle Foundation

For additional copies, write:
The Riehle Foundation
P.O. Box 7
Milford, OH 45150-0007 USA

Library of Congress Catalog Card No: 97-069725

ISBN: 1-877678-49-X

All biblical references were taken from the ST. JOSEPH BIBLE.
Front cover illustration: *The Creation of the Planets*
                    Michelangelo, Sistine Chapel
Cover designed by: **Christian Wilhelmy**

Table of Contents

Preface

The book of Genesis is the entrance to the Bible. The book has two distinct parts. The first part consists of eleven chapters that treat the origin of the world, of man, of sin, and of the chosen people. The second part, the remaining chapters (12-50), tells the stories of the patriarchs: Abraham, Isaac, Jacob and Joseph.

The first eleven chapters relate in simple and figurative language some fundamental truths of salvation history. The author did not intend to write a scientific work. Thus he uses the concepts of the time, but always aided by divine inspiration that eliminates all error. Though some of the truths taught in Genesis may seem commonplace now, we must remember that no book in the ancient world ever approximated the religious profundity of Genesis.

Three of these first eleven chapters tell of the origin of the world, of man, and of sin. The remaining eight portray the cosmic dimensions of sin. Scripture is called Salvation History. These eleven chapters tell why salvation is necessary. They tell us what sin is. They tell how it abounded and got a viselike stranglehold on the human race that no man could break. Somebody had to come, stronger than Satan, to break his power over mankind (*Mark* 3:27).

In chapter twelve God calls a man Abram; Salvation History begins. These remaining chapters of Genesis—from chapter twelve to fifty are historical in the sense that the events they narrate can be inserted into the civilization of the twentieth and nineteenth centuries B.C. These accounts were first transmitted by word of mouth and then written. The author was not interested in political events, but with families: births, marriages, deaths, often having religious significance.

He tells the origin of Israel through the stories of the patriarchs. The patriarchs were heads of clans, nomads living in tents, often near city-gates. The patriarch was the uncontested head of the clan. Polygamy was tolerated. The eldest son enjoyed the birthright; but to be official, it had to be ratified by the father. Fecundity was an honor, hospitality, a sacred duty.

Morality was very advanced but still imperfect: the patriarchs were great, but not without weaknesses; they grew in goodness.

Feast of the Visitation
May 31, 1997

Chapter 1

The Creation of the World
(Genesis 1)

The book of Genesis introduces the Pentateuch.[1] The name "Genesis" was given to this book by the Jews of Alexandria who translated the Old Testament from Hebrew into Greek, which became known as the Septuagint. The name Genesis was chosen because it was a book of beginnings, and the word "genesis" means "beginnings" or "origins" just as our words "genetics" or "genealogy."

Genesis tells of the origins of the world (Chapter 1), of man (Chapter 2), of evil (Chapters 3-11), and of the chosen people (Chapters 12-50). And though Genesis was not the first book written in the Pentateuch, it was put first because of its subject matter: Origins.

Genesis, like the rest of the Pentateuch, is a composite of four traditions that grew up around Moses.

1. **"In the beginning when God created the heavens and the earth."** Nothing is said of when the creation took place; it could have been a few thousands or many millions of years ago.

"In the beginning," that is, when all things began to be, God did not begin. He already existed; He was eternal. No need to prove the existence of God. *The heavens declare the glory of God, and the firmament proclaims his handiwork (Psalms* 19:2). *The fool says in his heart, 'There is no God' (Psalms* 14:1). We might just as well say that the watch has no watchmaker; the building no builder; the echo no voice; the footprint no foot; the smoke no fire; as to

---

[1] See Appendix 1: The Pentateuch.

1

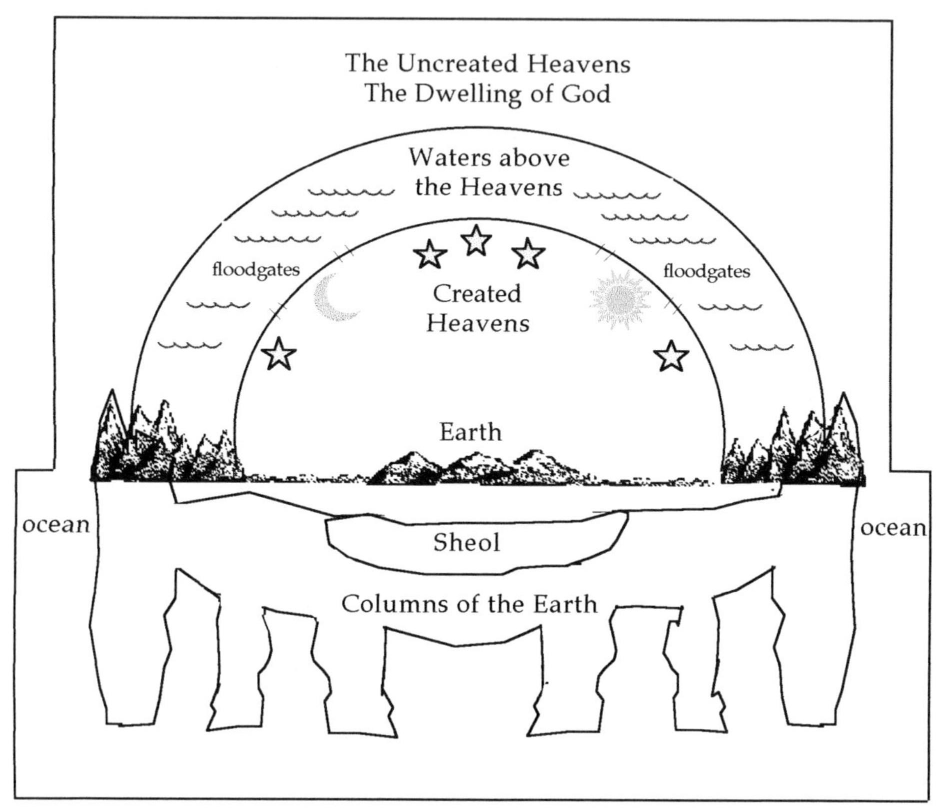

The World of the Hebrews

say—after viewing all the earth—that there is no God (*Catechism of the Catholic Church—CCC—#286*).

It was God who in the beginning created the heavens and the earth. So, in the Creed, we say, "I believe in God, the Father Almighty": Father, because He is the creator; and Almighty, because creation means to call into existence something out of nothing, an act of infinite power. There is a vast difference between making and creating: to make means to fashion or form something out of materials already existing; to create means to call into existence something out of nothing. A carpenter makes a chair out of wood; but he cannot create the wood (*CCC* #296-298).

2. And what did God create in the beginning? He **"created the heavens and the earth."** We might liken the world to a three-story building: the first floor is the earth; the second floor is the created heavens; and the third floor is the uncreated heavens where God dwells.

In the created heavens God put the angels. Like us, they too had to win a place in the uncreated heavens. Some of them failed; they rebelled against God, and they were cast out of the created heavens into Hell and became devils or bad angels. *Then war broke out in heaven; Michael and his angels battled against the dragon . . . the ancient serpent known as the devil or Satan . . . and they lost their place in heaven* (*Revelation* 12:7-9).

Hell was created for them. As Jesus will say to the wicked on Judgment Day: *Depart from me, you accursed, into the eternal fire prepared for the devil and his angels* (*Matthew* 25:41). Hell was not meant for us. Hell was not in the original creation. Hell came into existence as a result of the rebellion of Lucifer and some of the other angels.

Perhaps that rebellion explains why the author of Genesis writes: *The earth was a formless wasteland, and darkness covered the abyss.* We find it hard to believe that

God's original creation of the earth was a wasteland covered by darkness. The original creation, it would seem, would have to reflect something of the glory, perfection, order, and beauty of the Creator. Isaiah declares as much:

> *For thus says the Lord,*
> *The creator of the heavens, who is God,*
> *The designer and maker of the earth*
>   *who established it,*
> *Not creating it to be a waste, but*
>   *designing it to be lived in (Isaiah 45:18).*

Much later, perhaps thousands of years after the original creation of the earth, some terrible catastrophe must have happened that reduced the earth to a formless wasteland, put out its lights and covered her with darkness. Very likely the war between the angels could have reduced the earth to such a chaotic state, just as wars often do to countries.

3. Then to bring order out of chaos, the Spirit of God (a mighty wind swept over the waters) and the Word of God (Then God said) set out to remove the chaos and restore what had fallen into ruin, to make the earth habitable for man. Thus creation is the work of the Trinity: God the Father, Creator, who in the beginning made all things with His two hands: the Holy Spirit (a mighty wind) and His Son, the Word (Then God said) (*CCC* #291-292).

4. Genesis describes the restoration of the world in the framework of a week. The first step in any restoration is to clean up the debris, remove the rubble. So on the first three days, God separates light from darkness; the waters above the earth from the waters on the earth, by a dome; and the waters on the earth from the dry land, which He covered with plants and fruit trees.

Once the house was ready, God, on the next three days, put in the furnishings and the people. First, He hung lights in the dome: sun, moon, and stars. However, Genesis doesn't name the two great lights sun and moon because pagans worshipped the sun and moon. It simply refers to them as a greater and a lesser light and gives them the humble task of marking time. Next God put birds in the air and fish in the waters. Then He made animals and finally man. On the seventh day He rested, as if to teach man to observe the Sabbath rest and to remind him to help in the work of creation.

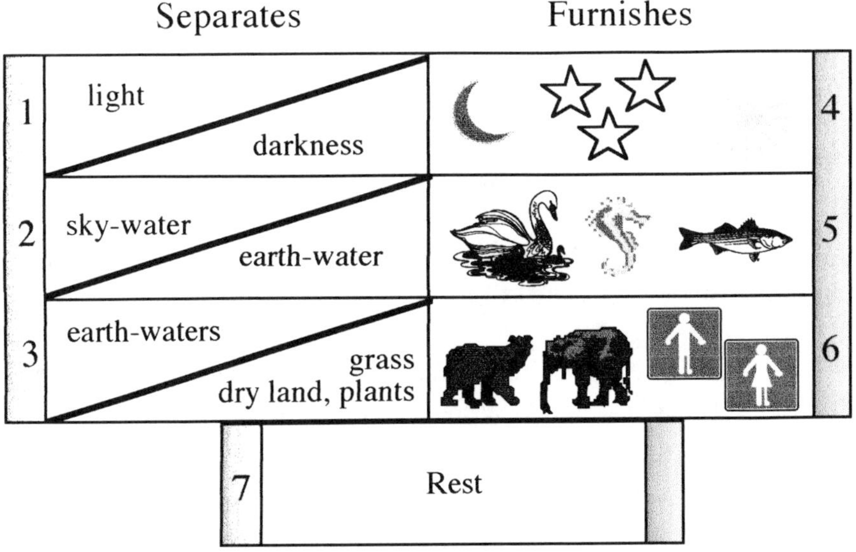

5. **Is there a clash between faith and science in the creation story as told by Genesis?** Faith says, "God created the heavens and the earth." It does not say **how**. Let science discover that. Faith says, "God is a God of order,

not chaos." Let science confirm this by discovering the laws and order that are built into the physical universe.

Daniel C. Matt in his book *God and the Big Bang* says the sun is five billion years old. Other scientists opine that creation took place at least twenty billion years ago. So what? A prestigious British physicist, Edmund Whittaker, in his book *The Beginning and the End* wrote: "It is simpler to postulate creation ex nihilo—the Divine will constituting Nature from nothingness." Edward Milne, a British theorist, concluded in his treatise on Relativity, "As the first cause of the universe…our picture is incomplete without Him (God)."

Our Holy Father, Pope John Paul II, in his message to the Pontifical Academy of Sciences (October 22, 1996) pointed out that it is better to talk about "theories of evolution" rather than a single theory. Also the Pope quoted Pius XII who stressed this essential point: "If the human body takes its origin from pre-existent living matter, the spiritual soul is immediately created by God." And it is by virtue of his spiritual soul that a human being is made human.

All we must believe is that God created everything. How and when He did it is for science to discover.

James Weldon Johnson (1871-1938), a black poet, in his poem *The Creation* describes creation in the style used by many black preachers.

> And God stepped out on space,
> And He looked around and said:
> I'm lonely—
> I'll make me a world.
>
> And far as the eye of God could see
> Darkness covered everything,
> Blacker than a hundred midnights
> Down in a cypress swamp.

Then God smiled,
And the light broke,
And the darkness rolled up on one side,
And the light stood shining on the other,
And God said: That's good!

Then God reached out and took the light in his hands,
And God rolled the light around in His hands
Until He made the sun;
And He set that sun a-blazing in the heavens.
And the light that was left from making the sun
God gathered it up in a shining ball
And flung it against the darkness,
Spangling the night with the moon and stars.
Then down between
The darkness and the light
He hurled the world;
And God said: That's good!

Then God himself stepped down—
And the sun was on His right hand,
And the moon was on His left;
The stars were clustered about His head,
And the earth was under His feet.
And God walked, and where He trod
His footsteps hollowed the valleys out
And bulged the mountains up.

Then He stopped and looked and saw
That the earth was hot and barren.
So God stepped over to the edge of the world
And he spat out the seven seas—
He batted His eyes, and the lightnings flashed—
He clapped His hands, and the thunders rolled—
And the waters above the earth came down,
The cooling waters came down.

Then the green grass sprouted,
And the little red flowers blossomed,
The pine tree pointed his finger to the sky,
And the oak spread out his arms,
The lakes cuddled down in the hollows of the ground,
And the rivers ran down to the sea;
And God smiled again,
And the rainbow appeared,
And curled itself around His shoulder.

Then God raised His arm and He waved His hand
Over the sea and over the land,
And He said: Bring forth! Bring forth!
And quicker than God could drop His hand,
Fishes and fowls
And beasts and birds
Swam the rivers and the seas,
Roamed the forest and the woods,
And split the air with their wings.
And God said: That's good!

Then God walked around,
And God looked around
On all that He had made.
He looked at His sun,
And He looked at His moon,
And He looked at His little stars;
He looked on His world
With all its living things,
And God said: I'm lonely still.

Then God sat down—
On the side of a hill where He could think;
By a deep, wide river He sat down;
With His head in His hands,
God thought and thought,
Till He thought: I'll make me a man!

Up from the bed of the river
God scooped the clay;
And by the bank of the river
He kneeled Him down;
And there the great God Almighty
Who lit the sun and fixed it in the sky,
Who flung the stars to the most far corner of the night,
Who rounded the earth in the middle of His hand;
This Great God,
Like a mammy bending over her baby,
Kneeled down in the dust
Toiling over a lump of clay
Till He shaped it in His own image;

Then into it He blew the breath of life,
And man became a living soul. Amen. Amen.

Note: The Babylonian and Greek Creation stories.

The creation story in Genesis is marvelously concise. One verse suffices to speak of the original creation. Another of the awful chaos into which the earth was plunged. Then less than thirty verses tell of the restoration in six days.

All the literary geniuses, historians, poets, or philosophers in the world could not have written anything that equals the creation narrative of the first chapter of Genesis. It is terse, yet comprehensive; simple, yet profound; exact, yet not technical. It stands unrivaled in the whole realm of literature.

The creation stories in the Babylonian and Greecian myths are vastly inferior to Genesis.

The Babylonian story of creation is in the *Enuma Elish*. According to this myth, in the beginning was chaos, the sea, a formless monster which is hostile to the land and perpetually attacks it. The chaos is personified by two deities, the male deity Apsu and the female deity Tiamat. From these two come the other gods and goddesses. One of these Marduk slays Tiamat after a titanic struggle and from her carcass forms the earth. (Heidel, Alexander. *The Babylonian Genesis.*)

According to the Greeks, in the beginning there was a black-winged bird Nyx. Nyx laid an egg. The egg hatched and out of it came Eros, the god of love. The upper part of the eggshell became Uranus, the heavens; the lower part became Gaia, the earth. Eros unites heaven and earth and from their union came the Titan gods and goddesses. From the Titans came the Olympian gods.

Edith Hamilton in her book *Mythology* wrote: "The Greeks did not believe that the gods created the universe. It was the other way about; the universe created the gods. Before there were gods heaven and earth had been formed.

They were the first parents. The Titans were their children and the (Olympian) gods were their grandchildren" (p. 24).

How sublimely superior is the Genesis account. In Genesis, God does not spring from the earth; the earth comes from God. In Genesis only God is eternal; heaven and earth had a beginning. In creating the heavens and the earth, there is no struggle; God is alone in solitary splendor and simply by a word He brings cosmos out of chaos (in Hebrew, tehom). The authors of Genesis, no doubt, were playing on the sound of the words: tiamat and tehom.

Chapter 2

The Creation of Man and Woman
(Genesis 2)

1. The creation of man according to the Priestly tradition (*Genesis* 1:26-27). Three times in this account (around 600 B.C.), God says, *Let us make man according to our image and likeness.* God is love. Love is a relational quality. As you cannot clap with one hand, so you cannot love unless there is another one to love. It takes two to tango, two to tangle, and two persons to love: the lover and the beloved. That was why God created man "male and female" so that man could love as God loves.

Furthermore, the one God is a community of loving Persons. To image that unity and community, God instituted marriage: where two persons become one body as God is one and where they can be fertile and multiply and become many persons, like the one God in three Persons.

2. The creation of man according to the Yahwist tradition (around 950 B.C.). The Priestly account of creation breaks off at Genesis 2:4a. At that point the authors introduce the Yahwist tradition. The Priestly account described God's creation in six days; the Yahwist account is used to describe only the creation of man from clay, his rise, his fall, and his hope for redemption.

The Yahwist account anthropomorphizes God. It likens God to a Potter. Pottery-making was one of the oldest industries known to man. God takes water and clay and fashions the mud into the form of a man, as a potter would shape clay into a vase. Then it likens God to a Glass Blower, another ancient industry. Pygmalion-like, God falls in love with His clay mold and blows into the nostrils of the clay mold the breath of life.

St. Paul uses this image to answer those who challenge God and ask, *Why have you created me so?*

Does not the potter, he replied, *have a right over the clay, to make out of the same lump one vessel for a noble purpose, and another for an ignoble one? (Romans* 9:21). Also, the Church uses the same image every Ash Wednesday when, putting ashes on one's forehead, she says, "Remember man you are dust."

Even though the Yahwist account is older than the Priestly account, Genesis puts it in Chapter Two rather than making it Chapter One, precisely because pagans at the time of the editing of the Pentateuch (around fifth century B.C.) were debunking their own myths about the gods and goddesses. Socrates was sentenced to death because he questioned the Grecian myths.

The editors of Genesis feared that, if God were presented as a Potter and Glass Blower in the first Chapter, the pagans would be turned off and would read no further, thinking that the God of Israel was no different from their own mythological deities. So they began Genesis with the Priestly account, which depicts God as totally different from humans—a powerful being way out there whose very word had creative power.

Did God actually create man by molding him out of clay and breathing into him the breathe of life? Of course not! God has neither hands, nor mouth. The story is pure imagery. What then were the authors of Genesis trying to tell us?

Well, from their experience the authors of Genesis saw man for what he really is—a Dr. Jekyll and a Mr. Hyde. They saw man kill man: Cain kill Abel, Lamech kill a youth, and man sin so much as to bring on the Flood. But they also saw something divine in man: his composing psalms, like

David, and writing words of wisdom, like Solomon. So they concluded there was something of the earth in man and something of the divine in him, that he has an earthy element in himself and also a godly element, something material and something spiritual. When the Church absorbed Greek culture, she spoke of these two elements in terms of body and soul.

3. The creation of woman. According to the pagans, women were on a level with chattel, with things. They were considered little more than beasts of burden or playthings to give pleasure, like those locked up in the harems of kings.

But the authors of Genesis, inspired by God, could never conceive of woman like that. She is not an animal. In fact, after man names the animals he is sad, because there is no one like himself. So man is put to sleep (a way of saying that he didn't really know how woman originated). However, Genesis describes her as being drawn from **man**. That was a powerful way of teaching that she had the same nature as man, for any child has the nature of its parent.

Then, she is pictured as formed from **man's side**, not from his head, for she was not to dominate him; nor from his feet, for he was not to dominate her; but from his side, for she was to be close to his heart and to walk beside him as his equal and helper in the journey of life.

She differed from man, but the difference was not antagonistic but complementary. She and man differed as the violin differs from the bow that draws music from it. Or in the words of Longfellow in *The Song of Hiawatha:*

> As unto the bow the cord is,
> So unto the man is woman,
> Though she bends him, she obeys him,
> Though she draws him, yet she follows,
> Useless each without the other!

Thus when the first man saw the first woman, he went into ecstasy and cried out, *This one at last is bone of my bones and flesh of my flesh* (not like any of the other animals). And *that is why a man leaves his father and mother and clings to his wife, and the two of them become one body.* With woman, earth became truly a paradise for man.

This break with the ideas about women current at the time (about 520 B.C.)—that she was not chattel, but man's equal and that she was not a mere object for man's pleasure but his partner in a marriage that was monogamous—had to come from above, had to be inspired by God. Such lofty ideas could not have come from man himself for man is so much a part of his surroundings that it was morally impossible for him to rise above them without help from above.

This monogamous marriage that united the first man and woman was indissoluble, for they formed one body. To break the sacred bond seemed to them as inconceivable as tearing limb from limb in one's body. How startling that must have been to the polygamous world of that day (cp. *Matthew* 19:8). The first man to take two wives was a murderer and a blasphemer, named Lamech (*Genesis* 4:19). This happened many, many generations after the creation of man; and Genesis points out that this action was a terrible deviation from God's original plan.

4. In this story is there room for the evolutionary process? Yes, if we admit two things: (1) that God started the evolutionary process; and (2) that evolution is restricted solely to the body. God creates the soul directly. But He could allow the body to evolve from lower forms, till it is ready for a soul. However, we must remember that evolution is still a theory and that the missing link is still missing.

5. Why did God make man? For happiness. St. Bonaventure explains that God created all things "not to increase His glory, but to show it forth and communicate it." Vatican Council One says, "God of His own goodness . . .(created) not for attaining his perfection, but in order to manifest this perfection through the benefits which he bestows on creatures . . ." (*CCC* #293). St. Iraeneus said God created man as the object upon whom He could confer His blessings.

Thus after creating man, God put him in a Garden of Eden. He shared with him His creative power: *Be fertile and multiply; fill the earth.* He shared with him His dominion: all creation is put under man—he names the animals as a sign he rules them. Thus from the beginning, God showed His good will toward man. When man falls, God does not abandon him. No, He clothes man and promises a Redeemer (*Genesis* 3:15).

Our Lord said that Hell was prepared for the devil and his angels (*Matthew* 25:41)—not for man! And just before that remark, He said that from the foundation of the world, God prepared a heavenly kingdom for man! (*Matthew* 25:34). Heaven, not Hell, is man's destiny—so great is God's love for us!

6. What does the story of Genesis tell us about the first man and woman? The first man and woman were never infants nor adolescents. God made them full grown, for they were able to take orders and to till and care for the Garden.

Made to the image and likeness of God, man differed from all the brute animals; in fact, he named them (*Genesis* 2:20), thus showing his superiority. But probably they did not have exceptional knowledge because later both would eat the forbidden fruit in an attempt to gain higher knowledge. The development of arts and crafts was left to future generations.

They were not inclined to evil, for . . . *he and his wife were both naked and they felt no shame.*

They were immortal, for the penalty of eating the forbidden fruit was to be death.

In the Garden, in addition to ordinary trees, pleasant to look at and good for food, there were two other mysterious trees: the tree of life and the tree of the knowledge of good and evil. Man was not only to till and care for the garden, he was also supposed to live responsibly under an authority greater than himself.

The phrase "good and evil" simply meant everything. It is like our expression "from A to Z." Man is warned that he is limited, he doesn't know everything, he isn't Mr. Know-it-all. The forbidden fruit is that man must not try to go it alone; he must not try to set up his own standards of morality; he must not declare his independence of God. To attempt this, God warned, was to spell out death not only for himself, but for all his descendants.

Finally, Genesis tells us that the first man and woman were in God's good graces, for God had put them in His garden. In ancient times, only friends of the king could walk in the king's garden.

The Garden of Eden was a garden of delights, where once all was harmony. It was a veritable Camelot. The climate was perfect all the year. There was simply not a more congenial spot for happ'ly-ever-aftering than in Camelot—the Garden of Eden.

" . . . the Garden of Eden . . . was situated in the plain of Mesopotamia . . . . There is an ancient tradition that Adam and Eve went to Palestine after they had fallen, and that they were buried at Calvary. This tradition is supported by private revelation." "According to the latest evidence from all sources, 20,000 years are quite sufficient to account for all that happened since the time of Adam and Eve" (Connell, Fr. Patrick. *Science of Today and the Problems of Genesis,* p. 341).

Chapter 3

The Fall of Man
(Genesis 3)

1. Why evil? The Jews believed and taught that their God was all good. Yet pagans always asked the question, "If your God is so good, how did evil—sickness, suffering, and death—come into the world? Why is man prone to evil?"

When Genesis was being edited, the Jews were in contact with the Persian Empire. Cyrus the Great was its king and a man named Zoroaster (c. 550 B.C.) was his friend. Zoroaster explained evil in the world by teaching that in the beginning there were two gods: a good one (Mazda, the god of light) and a bad one (Ahriman, the god of darkness). Ahriman, he taught, caused all the evils in the world.

The fiercely monotheistic Jews could not, and would not, countenance such dualism. The Jews had their own answer. Inspired by God, Genesis said, *The world was not always evil.* In fact, after each creation, seven times, Genesis writes that God *saw how good it was.* Actually, the world in the beginning was a paradise, a garden of delights. Man had it so good, Genesis writes, that a fallen angel had to enter the garden to bring in evil.

2. How, then, did evil enter the world? Evil, Genesis teaches, came not from a good God (*Sirach* 15:11-13), but from a man prodded by a fallen angel, who was no god, but a mere creature pictured as a snake (*Wisdom* 2:24; *Revelation* 12:9).

In describing the fall of man, Genesis used pagan symbols as stage props; for instance: a snake, a garden, and a tree. When movie directors make a Dracula picture, do they not also use stereotyped props: a black coach, a graveyard, a Gothic castle, eerie woods surrounding it, an inky black night, stormy winds and lightning, and so on?

Likewise, Genesis in describing how evil came into the world used a garden, a tree, and a snake. A snake was the symbol of the Canaanite fertility cults which were orgies that took place under trees situated in gardens in high places. Genesis was teaching that the false cults were not only evil but led to evil.

Also serpent worship was rampant in the ancient world. Even the Pharaohs of Egypt wore a serpent in their crowns as the symbol of life and fertility. In sharp contrast, Genesis presents the serpent as the instrument of death.

Genesis doesn't tell us that the serpent is the devil; later it is identified as the devil (*Wisdom* 2:24; *John* 8:44; *Revelation* 12:9). The serpent is anti-God. It addresses the woman first because she had not heard God's command (*Genesis* 2:17). Also, the authors are lashing out against the fertility cults. In countless excavations, figurines of many-breasted females have turned up; the female organs of productivity and fertility are fantastically exaggerated to show that the sex faculties had been made the object of worship—the source of sin.

The serpent is subtle and asks a simple question as if prompted by natural curiosity, *Did God really tell you not to eat from any of the trees in the garden?* Then it denies God's veracity. *You certainly will not die!* Finally, it levies the monstrous insinuation that God fears man's potential. Thus the serpent arouses the woman's desire; her senses do the rest: "She saw . . . she took some of its fruit and ate it . . . she gave some to her husband . . . and he ate it."

There is no mention of an "apple" in Genesis. This was wrongly introduced into popular thought by a mistranslation of the *Song of Songs* (8:5). Man's first sin did not consist in plucking a fruit from a forbidden tree. The sin consisted in man assuming he had the right to determine morality, to judge for himself what is right and what is wrong.

So, Genesis explains that evil came into the world through a disobedient man and a fallen angel, who enters the stage of history like a snake. Both had rebelled against the good God and unloosed a Pandora's box of evils upon the entire world.

3. The lessons of man's fall. The fall of man teaches us first that there is an angelic power at work in the world seeking the harm of man. He is a cunning liar, crafty as a serpent. Jesus described him, the devil, as a liar and a murderer (*John* 8:43-44).

Man's fall also teaches that in temptation it is well to resist beginnings. The woman erred in answering the serpent. Then, too, she did not realize the power of suggestion, that evil can enter through the eyes. *The woman saw that the tree was good for food, pleasing to the eyes.*

Finally, the fall teaches us never to underestimate the power of a woman. A woman is a power for good or for evil. She can make a man out of a fool or a fool out of a man. The woman *took some of its fruit and ate it; and she also gave some to her husband, who was with her, and he ate it.*

4. The original sin. The sin of the first man and woman was a mortal sin of disobedience, springing from a pride nutured by the devil. (cp., *Roman* 5:19; CCC #397). It was a very serious sin for the penalty was death; moreover, it affected the entire human race and occasioned all the evils in the world to this very day.

5. The effect of the sin of the first man and woman on themselves. When the man and woman sinned, they lost practically everything. God curses the serpent, but not the man nor the woman. In cursing the serpent, God spoke of a long and bitter conflict between the serpent and his descendants and the woman and her descendants. For neither of the combatants was there to be immediate and complete victory. Yet, like a snake, the tempter shall bite the dust; that is, he shall be humbled by having his head crushed by the seed of the woman (*Genesis* 3:15).

As for the man and the woman, they lost their **innocence**, their inner harmony. They felt shame, and so they covered their physical nakedness with fig leaves to prevent the stirring of the flesh against the spirit.

The fig leaves represented a second failure of man: the attempt to hide his sin. Thus when the first man and woman heard the voice of God, they hid themselves. "Conscience doth make cowards of us all." They felt guilt so they hid from God and lost their **intimacy** with Him.

So many foolishly either seek to excuse their sins or to deny them instead of confessing them to God through a priest and receiving absolution. God gave the first man a chance to confess his sin: *Who told you that you were naked? Man* could have confessed his guilt; but no, he excused himself and blamed the woman, and even God. Notice what the man's answer was, *The woman whom You put here with me*—he infers that God too is at fault, for he says, *The woman whom* **YOU** *put here* . . . . The woman in turn blamed the serpent. "Passing the buck" is a game as old as the human race. But it is of no avail.

God punishes the man and the woman and their children in their fundamental roles in life. The woman's role is motherhood; after the first sin, she is condemned to bring forth children in pain; and *"your urge shall be for your husband, and he shall be your master"* (*Genesis* 3:16). *Man immediately shows his mastery by naming his wife and calling her "Eve"* (*Genesis* 3:20). The man's role is to be provider; but after his sin, the earth fights against him, and only by the sweat of his brow can he get bread to eat.

The final punishment was death. *You are dirt and to dirt you shall return.* They were expelled from Eden. And to prevent them access to the tree of life that would forestall death, the cherubim were stationed before it, and between them a sword flaming zigzag lightning barred the way to the tree of life.

6. The effects of the sin of our first parents on their children, the human race. Every child is born with original sin now; that is, the child is born without sanctifying grace, with a strong tendency to sin, and subject to sickness, suffering, and death.

Thus today man flees from God. Why? Everything else seeks the source of its life: the child goes to its mother, the sunflower turns to the sun, and the roots grow toward the water—all beings move to the source of their life. Only man does not. That is a fact. Thompson in his great poem "The Hound of Heaven" pictures man as running away from God and God pursuing him as a hound does its prey. "I fled him down the nights and down the days . . . . " Why? Why does man flee from God, the source of his life? Genesis says it is because of man's first sin, for after his sin man experienced guilt and so hid himself from God.

Thus today man finds it easier to do evil than to do good. To do evil is like swimming with the current; to do good is like swimming against the current. This is so, because man lost his inner harmony after sin. His passions were no longer subject to his reason, and his reason was no longer subject to his will, and his will no longer subject to his God. His rebellion against God led to the rebellion of his passions against himself. Thus the flesh lusts against the spirit. That was why man after his sin, clothed himself; his nakedness aroused shame and bad desires. Mark Twain wrote that "man is the only animal who blushes or needs to."

How wrong Rousseau was in his book *Emile*. He taught that the child is born morally good. Therefore, in education Rousseau advocated that the child be given free rein to his natural tendencies and that all forms of discipline, formal training, and restrictions in general be avoided in education.

C. S. Lewis in his book *The Abolition of Man* stated that such education, without moral and spiritual values, produces only clever devils. For, as St. Augustine said, "We are like wounded soldiers, striving to rise, destined to fall." And fall we most assuredly will, without discipline and training, and the help of God's graces.

William Golding confirms the same truth in his book *The Lord of the Flies*. His book repudiates the theory of socialist philosophers who teach that all the ills that man is heir to, are attributable solely to heredity and environment. Our first parents had perfect heredity: they came directly from God; and perfect environment: they lived in a paradise. Yet they fell. The trouble with mankind is not something external, but something internal. Man needs the grace of God. Without it, as the uncultivated garden goes to weeds, so shall the undisciplined child.

After man's sin, all men sought redemption, a savior, so they offered sacrifice. Genesis shows that religion was but man's effort to regain what he had lost. In the Garden of Eden, man was in God's good graces. He was His intimate friend and walked, so to speak, with Him. But by sin man was disgraced: he lost the divine friendship, became ME-centered instead of God-centered—was stripped NAKED of all God's blessings. Cardinal Wolsley, when he had fallen out of the good graces of King Henry VIII, said to Cromwell, "Had I but serv'd my God with half the zeal I serv'd my king, he would not now in mine age have left me naked to mine enemies."

We speak of the work of Jesus as redemption. "Redemption" means to "restore" to win back for us what once we had. What we once had, must have been divine life. For Jesus said, *I am come that you may have life.* The life Jesus was talking about couldn't have meant human life for His hearers already had that, they weren't corpses. Besides human life, Jesus had divine life. He must have meant, not human life, but this other kind of life that He Himself enjoyed, divine life. Therefore we must once have had divine life. When, if not in our first parents, for no one after them had it?

7. The Immaculate Conception. Only one person was spared the terrible ravages of the original sin—Mary, the Mother of God. William Wordsworth in a sonnet wrote of Mary as "our tainted nature's solitary boast . . . purer than white foam in central ocean tost." The Church teaches that Mary was not only sinless, but that she was conceived even immaculate; that is, that she was full of grace from the very first moment that she was conceived in the womb of her good mother, St. Anne.

HIS MASTERPIECE

An artist conceived a great picture,
Yet feared after all his toil
That even the whitest background
His masterpiece would spoil.

So he sought for a spotless canvas;
He would paint on a fadeless scroll.
And away in an unknown village
He found it—a virgin soul!

So He took all the blue of the heavens,
He took all the gold of the sun,

> With the hundred hues of the rainbow,
> And He mixed them into one.
>
> He sought all the beauty of Nature,
> He bought all the glory of Grace,
> And etched with His brush on the canvas
> The wealth of one Woman's face;
>
> And the whole world stood enraptured,
> And the angels sang for mirth,
> For His portrait was so perfect—
> It brought a God to earth.

The artist of course was God the Father. The Masterpiece He conceived was the Incarnation, His Son becoming Man. The canvas was Mary, made spotless by her Immaculate Conception.

Note: In 1854 the Church defined that "Mary, **from the first instant of her conception**, was preserved from any stain of original sin." But sin attaches to a person and not to a thing. Therefore, Mary was a person from conception. And so is everybody else. And that makes abortion, the taking of the life of a child in the womb, murder!

Chapter 4

Quicksand
(Genesis 4-11)

God had made the world good—oh, so good! Seven times, God said, "It was good!" Then sin came. It was sin that wrecked King Arthur's Camelot. Sin. After Lancelot and Guenevere had sinned, Guenevere bemoans the terrible consequences of their sin; "And now there's Twice as much grief; Twice the strain for us; Twice the despair; Twice the pain for us; as we had known before." It was sin too, that shattered God's beautiful creation, reduced it to a vale of tears, and caused man to lose the earthly paradise.

After the Fall, the author of Genesis, in Chapters four to eleven, took stories handed down by word of mouth over the centuries and put them together to teach that the first sin so inclined man to sin that he was like one in quicksand, unable to save himself.

The author took stories like those about Cain, Lamech, the Nephilim, the Flood, and the Tower of Babel.

These stories might be likened to the piers supporting the arches of a bridge. The span of the arches are the length of time between the stories. How long these spans were, or how many years intervened between the stories, is unknown. The best authorities hold that twenty thousand years are quite sufficient to account for all that happened since the time of Adam and Eve. The Cain and Abel story reflects the civilization around 8000 B.C., when farming and sheepherding arose. The crafts and arts at Lamech's time postulate a highly developed civilization belonging to the Bronze Age (3000 B.C.) and the Iron Age (1200 B.C.). Thus Cain and Abel were Adam's children in the same sense that we are, or in the sense Jesus was called the Son of David.

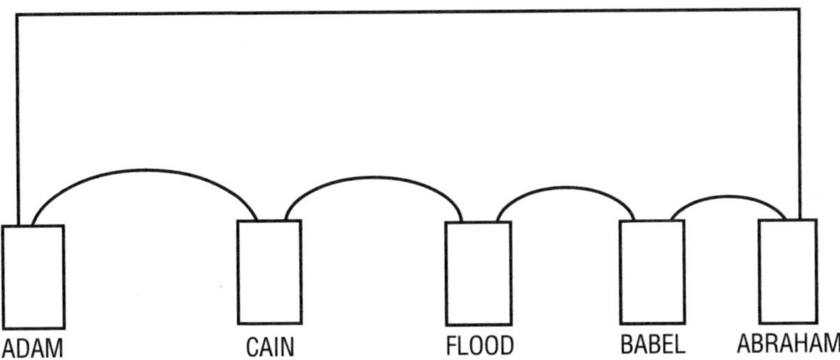

The author was not concerned with scientific data—all he wanted to teach was that after the first sin, man was like one caught in quicksand, from which he could not extricate himself. Instead, he sank deeper and deeper into sin. He was sin-bent.

As a person caught in quicksand can be saved only if someone from the outside helps—throws him a branch or a rope or pulls him out with a horse: so man trapped in the quicksand of sin needed help from outside himself—he needed a savior, a redeemer.

1. The Cain-Abel story.
The details of the Cain-Abel story, like sacrifice and worship, farming and cattle raising, reflect a civilization after the Flood, about 8000 B.C. So we have an anachronism here, using things out of their time period. But the purpose of the author of Genesis was not historical, but theological. He wished to show that the first sin led to sin after sin; that man needed outside help, a savior, a redeemer.

In the Cain-Abel story, the terrible sin of fratricide is committed. Self-assertion against God leads to self-assertion against man.

In some way (maybe by sending down fire on Abel's offering) God made it clear that He favored Abel and his offering. Cain, as a result, became resentful (angry) and crestfallen (envious). So God spoke to Cain through his conscience. Conscience reminded him that anger and envy are foolish things. "If you do well," conscience prompted, "You will not become crestfallen, but you will be able to hold your head up high. But if you do not change, watch out! Sin, like a wild beast crouches at your door and is ready to pounce on you and devour you. Still you are the master; which way you go depends on you" (cp. *Genesis* 4:4-7).

Cain turned a deaf ear to the voice of his conscience. He murdered his brother, Abel. But "murder will out," sin cannot remain hidden; Abel's spilt blood cries out to God. God confronts Cain, *Where's your brother?* Cain lies, *I do not know,* and then continues with the classic example of irresponsibility, *Am I my brother's keeper?*

Cain lies. He has no contrition. He makes no confession. He simply tries to cover up his guilt as our first parents did and as we so often do. Yet man cannot escape himself. Guilt haunts and taunts the sinner, like the Furies in the old Greek plays, driving him almost mad as he runs from place to place to flee the pangs of guilt. Thus Cain becomes a *restless wanderer on the earth* (*Jude* 12-13; *2 Peter* 2:17).

Still, all Cain can think of is the enormity of his punishment, not of his sin. He fears tribal revenge for his murder. But God assures him that the mark of his own clan (perhaps a tattoo mark) will prevent this. So, Cain goes far east from Eden, to the Land of Nod, the land of nomads and wanderers.

2. The Lamech story. Cain's family tree embraces seven generations. To guarantee his own protection, Cain abandoned the nomadic way of life and built a city, which he named after his son, Enoch. From Cain's line is born Lamech. His story is told to show that man is steadily sinking into the morass of sin. Lamech is the first man to commit bigamy—he takes two wives. In addition, he is a murderer—he kills a youth for bruising him. His song of the sword is the first piece of poetry quoted in the Bible. His swaggering and boasting comes after the forging of bronze and iron. With these weapons he feels he can exact seventy-fold vengeance—kill on the slightest provocation. His words breathe unbelievable defiance of God.

But all is not lost. With the birth of Seth, man gets a new start—another child *in place of Abel.* Seth begets Enosh. And men begin to invoke the Lord by name.

3. The Generations from Adam to Noah, the Pre-Flood Patriarchs (*Genesis* 5:1-32). Often in the Bible the genealogies are neither chronologies nor are they complete. The author merely gathered some ancient names: mighty men of the past (twenty in all) and arranged them systematically, ten here in Chapter 5 and ten in Chapter 11:10.

The terms "son," "daughter," and "begot" have a much wider use in the Semitic tongue than in the European; for instance, we call Christ the "Son of David," although David lived one thousand years before Christ.

The genealogy of Chapter 5 was meant to teach three things.

First, it aims at linking the line of God's people with Adam.

Secondly, it underscores the fact that God had not lied when He said to our first parents, *If you eat the forbidden fruit, you are surely doomed to die.* So eight times, this truth is pounded home by the hammer-like refrain "then he died."

Finally, the genealogy shows that sin was still on the march.

The gradual shortening of man's life span was a way of saying that man was becoming more and more wicked. The Jews had only a blurry concept of the afterlife. God, they felt, rewards man here and now. A long life is God's reward for a good life. The shortening of man's life span, therefore, was an indication of man's moral declension—the progress of sin.

Enoch stresses the same by opposite. Enoch does not die. The number 365 is a number of perfection based on the solar year and indicates moral perfection. The Bible says that Enoch *walked with God.* When two walk together, the supposition is they are in agreement, harmony, sympathy. Walking with God means taking His way and not one's own, going His way and not my way. To walk suggests steady progress—not a run or a leap or a spurt, but steady progress. Progress means forward movement toward a goal. Enoch walked with God; that is, he grew to do God's will more and more each day, until God stepped in and took him as He did Elijah.

The longevity of the patriarchs is not to be taken literally. Length-of-years-lived was an ancient Eastern device to fill a time gap and to show the importance, the greatness, of a person or people. If a mother asks her little child how much he loves her, the child might say, "A hundred million bushels." That is a child's way of saying, "I love you a whole lot." So the Sumerians and the Babylonians used large numbers to indicate the greatness of a people; and a long reign to indicate the greatness of a person. Thus the Babylonian king, Enmeduranna was said to have reigned seventy-two thousand years.

4. The Nephilim (*Genesis* 6:1-7). The sons of heaven could be simply the good people, the descendants of Seth, and the daughters of man could be the bad people, the descendants of Cain. The good and the bad began to intermarry. Evil associations corrupt good manners—thus the good were corrupted; the Sethites became as evil as the Cainites. *They took for their wives as many of them as they chose.*

From these unions sprang a race of giants, the Nephilim.

The giants here very probably do not refer to bodily stature, like the Titans in Grecian mythology, or like Polyphemus in the *Odyssey*. More likely, giants refer to moral qualities: men great in and renowned for their lawlessness, their violence, their cruelty; mighty in exploits of wrongdoing. Sin and immorality became so rife that God said, *In a hundred and twenty years, I will wipe out from the earth the men whom I have created.*

5. Noah. In the midst of all the wickedness in the world, there was one bright ray of hope in a man named Noah. He *found favor with the Lord,* for he was a good man, blameless in that age, for he walked with God, as Enoch had, and begot three sons: Shem, Ham, and Japheth. It is hard enough to be good among the good, but to be good among the wicked, the corrupt, the lawless, that is an achievement.

Make yourself an ark, God told Noah. The Hebrew word for ark is the same word as that used to describe the basket Moses was put in as a baby among the bullrushes. The ark was not meant to be a cruising hotel but simply a box that would float and could be used as a storage room. It was to be 440 x 73 x 44 feet and three stories high. Near the top of the ark, there was to be an open space on all sides to admit light and air. The construction of the ark was God's last warning; for this reason, Noah is called a *herald of righteousness* (*2 Peter* 2:5).

The story of the great Flood is a composite narration based on two separate sources interwoven like a patchwork quilt. This fact explains the doublets in the story, certain inconsistencies like the number of the various animals taken into the ark, and the timetable of the Flood.

For instance, one source has God telling Noah to bring into the ark two of all living creatures; while the other has God telling him to bring in seven pairs. The one source has the Flood caused by heavy rains for forty days and forty nights, which took twenty-one days to subside, so that it all lasted sixty-one days; whereas the other source has the rains fall for one hundred fifty days and nights, taking two hundred ten days to subside, so that the whole duration of the flood was three hundred sixty-five days. The author so respected his sources that he included both accounts.

The extent of the Flood. Geographically, it did not cover the whole earth. The Flood was serious, but local. First, all the species of animals, some 519,000, could not get into the ark. Also, to cover the highest mountaintops, for instance, Mt. Everest 29,141 feet high, would require water to rise five and one half miles above sea level on all points of the earth. To dispose of such a vast quantity of water would be a problem indeed.

The sacred author believed the Flood covered the whole earth, because his notion of the earth's size and makeup was very limited. In profane literature, the Flood tradition is not universal. It is unknown to the Egyptians, most Indo-Europeans, the Arabs, the Chinese, and the Japanese.

Anthropologically, the Flood was not universal, for thousands of years were required for the various languages of the Near East to develop.

The author was not interested in the scientific facts of the Flood, but in teaching religious lessons, namely, that sin was imbedded in the very nature of man and that God was just and merciful. God's justice is exemplified in the punishment of the wicked and the sparing of the just. His mercy is exemplified by His punishing the wicked by drowning and not by fire as at Sodom and Gomorrha. Fire is instantaneous; drowning is slow—it affords time to repent, especially if it takes forty or a hundred and fifty days. Furthermore, God in His mercy did not take away from man the power to procreate.

The aftermath of the Flood. Noah's first act after leaving the ark was to offer sacrifice. God's response was immediate. He promises not to curse the ground as after

Adam's sin. Instead, He blesses Noah and makes a covenant with him. This is the first covenant of God with man and our first encounter with the word "covenant." A covenant is a unilateral contract: God stipulates the terms; man is free to accept or reject them. Man's part is to respect human life, unlike Cain, and to be fertile and multiply. God, for His part, promises never again to destroy the earth by a flood. As a sign that He had set aside His anger which had beclouded His countenance and had let loose the Flood, God said, *I set my bow in the clouds.*

The bow was an instrument of war. How could it be a sign of peace? When a Choctaw Indian surrendered, he handed over to his conqueror his bow and arrow with the arrow pointing toward himself. Similarly, a gunslinger does the same thing when he surrenders to a sheriff: he hands over the gun with the barrel pointing toward himself. The bow in the clouds, the rainbow, has the arrow pointing toward God and not toward the earth, and so a sign of peace.

St. Peter used the Flood as a symbol of baptism (*1 Peter* 3:20-21). The Flood destroyed the wicked. Thus it prevented the good from being corrupted. The Psalmist said:

> *For the scepter of the wicked shall not rest*
> *Over the land of the just*
> *for fear the hands of the just should turn to*
> *evil* (*Psalm* 125).

The Ark saved Noah's body; but the Flood saved his soul.

Noah and his sons. Only one incident is narrated about Noah before his death—the story of his drunkenness.

Noah, a man of the soil, planted a vineyard. The potency of Palestinian wine is proverbial (*Isaiah* 16:8-10). Noah was unaware of this fact, so in testing the wine he had made, he became drunk; but not so drunk that he could not find his tent and go there to sleep it off.

Ham discovered his father in this state and ridiculed him. The Jews were very sensitive to impiety (*Deuteronomy* 27:16). So, Ham, the father of the Canaanites, is cursed. The story is meant to demean Israel's enemy, the Canaanites, and to justify the Israelites enslavement of the Canaanites, and to deter the Jews from following the foul sexual practices in the Canaanite religion that strongly attracted the Israelites.

6. The Table of the Nations (*Genesis* 10).

Like two-faced Janus, the Table of the Nations looks to the past and to the future. It is put here to show that Noah and his sons fulfilled God's command to increase and multiply. It witnesses to the vitality of the blessing given Noah. From this one man all the nations of the world are derived; all nations are one community sprung from the sons of Noah. The Table of Chapter 5 was genealogical: it shows that God's people were connected with Adam. The Table here of Chapter 10 is ethnological: it shows that all nations have a common origin from the sons of Noah.

The Table looks also to the future: from many nations to one nation. In the first verse of Chapter 10, the sons of Noah are listed as Shem, Ham, and Japheth. Yet in the rest of the Chapter they are treated in reverse order: Japheth, Ham, and Shem.

The sons of Japheth are put first in the Table as the least important to the readers for whom Genesis was written. They played only a slight part in Hebrew history. The Japhites dwelt to the north and west of Mesopotamia and Syria, on islands and peninsulas in the Mediterranean; they included the Medes, Greeks, Cypriotes, and inhabitants of Rhodes and the Aegean Isles.

The sons of Ham came next in the Table, because they had much more contact with Israel. The Hamites dwelt in northern Africa along the Nile and the coasts of the Red

Sea; they included the Ethiopians, Egyptians, Canaanites, Babylonians, Assyrians, and the Hittites.

A significant Hamite was Nimrod, probably Tukulti-Nimurta, thirteenth century B.C., the first Assyrian conqueror of Babylonia. He was a great builder and hunter, the two leading characteristics of Eastern monarchs as such. Assyrian monarchs are often pictured as great hunters.

Shem is put last in the Table, because the last place is the place of honor. This place was reserved for Shem because he is the ancestor of the Israelites. The Shemites dwelt between the Japhites and the Hamites, in Mesopotamia, Syria, and in Arabia. They included the Persians, Assyrians, Lydians, Syrians, and the descendants of Eber.

Eber is short for Eber-hannahar, the region on the other side of the river Euphrates, that is, Syria and Palestine. Shelah, Eber's father, probably gave this land to his son on the occasion of a tribal movement. Eber was an eponymous ancestor: an ancestor who gave his name to the group. Thus the Greeks or Hellenes traced their history back to Hellen. The Hebrews traced their history back to Eber. Cuneiform literature abounds in references to nomads called Habiru by settled folk. Abraham was probably a part of the Habiru. Gradually the name was confined to his descendants as "Hebrews."

Thus three roads lead from Noah to the whole wide world. Then two of them, the sons of Japheth and the sons of Ham, come to a dead end. They are dealt with first, then disposed of. The third road, that of the sons of Shem, leads on to Israel, the people of God. Politically, Israel, one of the nations, was the most insignificant of them all. Yet theologically, it was to be the nation through which all the other nations in the world would be blessed.

7. The Tower of Babel (*Genesis* 11:1-9). The Table of the Nations was meant to teach the basic family unity of all nations on earth. The story of the Tower of Babel explains how they became disunited.

The Tower of Babel is the symbol of man trying to build a city without God—the secular city! The Tower is not meant to teach the origin of languages. Language underwent a long, gradual process of development. The word "language" here is used figuratively to symbolize unity or disunity. For instance, we say, "You talk my language" which means we see "eye to eye." That the whole earth spoke one language meant that once mankind was unified economically, politically, and socially. But once sin entered, once man sought to live without God, it was then that division, fragmentation, entered into society. Men no longer spoke the same language; they no longer saw eye to eye; they became at odds with each other—they warred!

The Tower of Babel story was probably written about the eighth or ninth century B.C. shortly after the Kingdom of Solomon was split into two kingdoms. The Babel story was meant to point out that the real cause of civil discord is man's turning from God (to golden calves, as under Jeroboam).

8. The line from Shem to Abraham (*Genesis* **11:10-26**)**.** Closing these early chapters of Genesis is a last genealogy, tracing the descendants of Shem down to Abraham. Again, we see the selective process at work; only the descendants of Shem are given, those of Ham and Japheth disappear. This genealogy parallels that of Chapter 5. In both genealogies we have ten entries, and the formula is the same—*This is the record of. . . .* As in Chapter 5, longevity was definitely on the decline. The reduction of man's life span shows that the devastating role of sin is still at work. Man sinks deeper and deeper into the morass of sin and needs outside help.

9. The total effect of all the stories in *Genesis* **4 to 11.** One thing these stories show is the ripple effect of sin. As a stone thrown into water causes ripples that reach to the shore, so the first sin caused ripples—other sins.

- disobedience (1st sin)
- murder (Cain-Abel)
- polygamy (Lamech)
- promiscuity (Nephilim)
- disunity—war (Babel)

These stories also show that sin is in the blood of man. They show that the human race gets worse instead of better. They show that man is powerless to extricate himself from sin. They say loud and clear that man needs a liberator, a redeemer—somebody outside the human race to crush the serpent's head. That outside help comes when God Himself intervenes once again into history and calls Abraham. With this call, pre-history ends and history begins.

These first eleven chapters of Genesis are the doorway to the Bible. They "state the principal truths which are fundamental for our salvation and also give a popular description of the origin of the human race and the chosen people . . . . Whatever of the popular narrations have been inserted into the Scriptures, must in no way be considered on a par with myths or other such things" (*Humani Generis*, 8/12/50, #68-69; Denzinger, #2302). Myths are the figments of the imagination; the Scripture is the inspired word of God.

Genesis teaches these fundamental truths of salvation: man's divine origin, his nature, his relationship with God, his place in the universe, marriage, sin, and the evils consequent upon sin. In all this Genesis tells of the great and heartfelt relationship between God and man, which is basically the great love of the Creator for His creature—the Father for His children.[1]

---

[1] See Appendix 2: Biblical Timetable

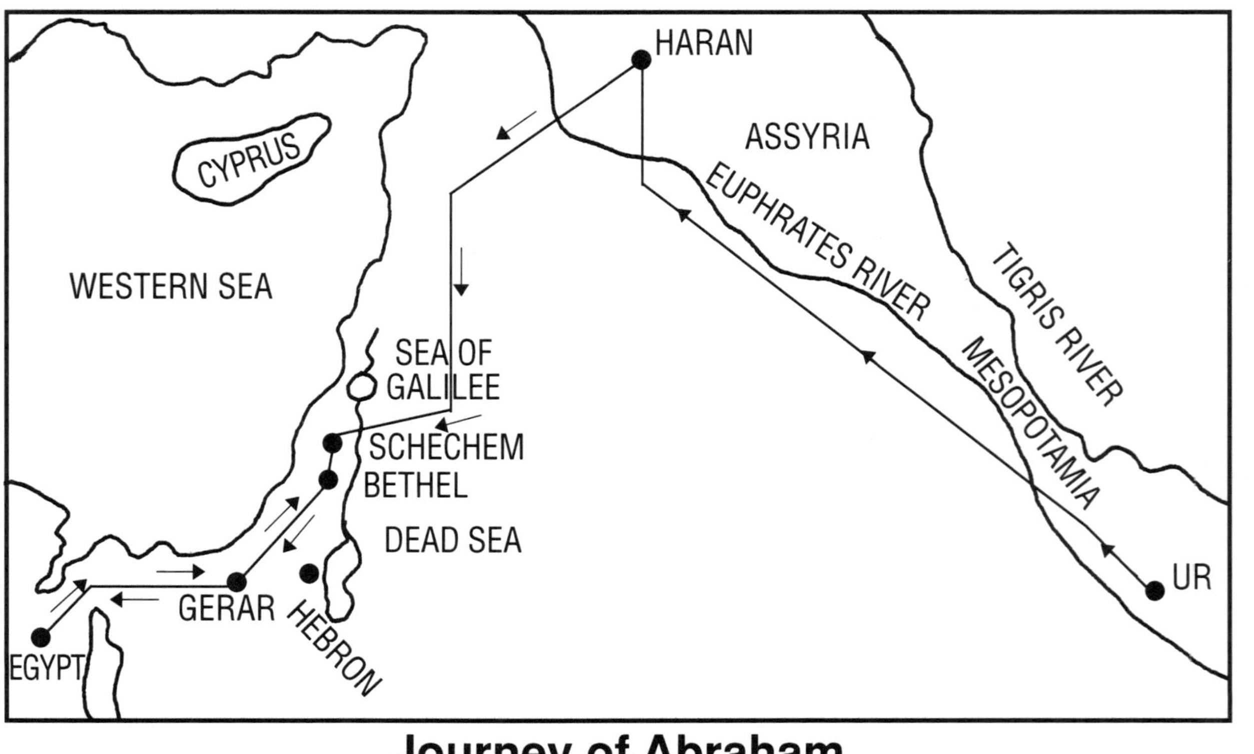

Journey of Abraham

Chapter 5

The Abraham Story

Genesis deals with origins: the origin of the world (Chapter 1); the origin of man (Chapter 2); the origin of sin (Chapter 3); the consequences of sin (Chapters 4-11); and finally, the origin of God's chosen people (Chapters 12-50).

Thousands of years before Christ, pagans had strange notions of God. Without divine revelation, how else could man fashion a god except after himself? Thus the pagans made their god after their own image and likeness. It was not good for man to be alone—he was male and female—so the pagans felt it was also not good for their god to be alone, so they created gods and goddesses. Man is self-centered, so they pictured their gods that way; dwelling high in the skies not caring a wit about mankind. They felt they had to reach these gods and appease them. So they built temple towers, skyscrapers, ziggurats, like the tower of Babel, and offered sacrifices to these gods.

Divine revelation, on the contrary, revealed that the true God is totally unlike these pagan concepts. First, He is one God, not many. Secondly, He cares about mankind. After sin, He does not abandon man, but promises him a redeemer (*Genesis* 3:15). After mankind hits rock bottom in sin, God steps into the picture on His own initiative and sets in motion man's redemption.

Genesis says, *The Lord said to Abram, 'Go forth from the land of your kinsfolk and from your father's house to a land that I will show you'* (*Genesis* 12:1). St. Stephen put it this way, *The God of glory appeared to our Father Abraham while he was in Mesopotamia* (*Acts* 7:2). Note that it was God who took the initiative: He spoke to Abram.

And He appeared to him. This was the first time since the Fall that God appeared to man. And He asked only one thing of Abram: faith!

Paradise had been lost through a lack of faith; it was to be regained by an act of faith. God told Abram to leave the land of his kinsfolk and go to a land *that I will show you.* God didn't tell him to what land he was to go. He simply said, *Go!* Then God went on to say, *I will make of you a great nation* (*Genesis* 12:2).

So Abram did as the Lord had directed. But his faith was not as yet perfect. God had told him to go forth from his father's house. Abram went forth from the land, but not from his father's house. He took Terah, his own father, with him and his nephew, Lot. Terah delayed Abram's going to Canaan for five years; and Lot, as we shall see, caused him many trials.

In journeying from his homeland, Abram followed the caravan route from Ur in the east to Haran in the west. At Haran, Abram stayed till his father died; then he journeyed on to Canaan. Only after his arriving there did God appear to Abram at Shechem and say, *To your descendants I will give this land* (*Genesis* 12:7). Hence it became known as the Promised Land.

In the Promised Land a famine occurred (*Genesis* 12:10-30). Again, instead of trusting God, Abram left for Egypt without so much as consulting God. As always, when we take things into our own hands, they sort of boomerang.

In Egypt, Abram concealed the fact that Sarai was his wife. Pharaoh set his heart on Sarai for she was very beautiful. To ingratiate himself to Abram, whom Pharaoh thought was Sarai's brother, Pharaoh lavished rich gifts upon him. *Abram received flocks and herds, male and female slaves, . . . asses, . . . camels* (*Genesis* 12:16). One of the female slaves was Hagar, given to Sarai. Hagar became a thorn in Sarai's side. Her child by Abram was

Ishmael, the father of the Ishmaelites, who became an enemy of God's people.

Then on his return to Canaan, Abram's vast herds made it necessary for him and Lot to part—*the land could not support them both* (*Genesis* 13:6). So with great generosity, Abram let his nephew Lot select the territory he desired and Abram was content to take what was left—Bethel.

The worldliness of Egypt seemed to have gotten into Lot's blood. For he chose the land among the cities of the Dead Sea basin, pitching his tents near Sodom. Even though the inhabitants of Sodom were very wicked, Lot did not seem to care—apparently all that mattered to him was the richness of the land. This was the beginning of his decline.

First he dwelt on the outskirts of Sodom, then in Sodom, and finally, after Abram had conquered the four kings of Mesopotamia who had ravaged Sodom, Lot became a somebody because of his uncle's deeds and ended up an alderman at the gates of Sodom. Both he and his daughters married Sodomites.

When the kings of the Dead Sea basin revolted against their Mesopotamian overlords, Chedorlaomer, the king of Elam, led the other kings allied with him to crush the revolt. Which they did. Lot was taken prisoner. When Abram heard of this, he mustered a small army and slew Chedorlaomer and the allied kings and freed his nephew. In victory, Abram stopped at Salem, probably Jerusalem, and was given bread and wine to eat by Melchizedek, king and priest of Salem. Abram gave Melchizedek a tenth of the booty he had recovered.

Later on, this Melchizedek became a type of the Messiah. He was a priest of one of the numerous Canaanite gods, El-Elyon, that is, the most high god. In a book filled with genealogies, Melchizedek is presented as being "without father, without mother"—a good type of the Messiah who is without beginning and without end. He was a priest of the most high God—a good type of the Messiah's universal priesthood in contrast to the Levitical priesthood, which existed only for the Israelites.

Melchizedek was King of Salem. "Melchi" means "king"; "zedek" means "justice"; and "Salem" means "peace." Thus Melchizedek further typified the Messiah who was to be a King who brings peace through fulfilling His Father's justice. Peace is the work of justice.

After Abram had defeated the four kings by a night attack, he naturally feared reprisals. However, the Lord reassured Abram, *Fear not, Abram! I am your shield.* The words *Fear not,* or their equivalent *Be not afraid,* occur almost one hundred eighty times in the Bible. And since Abram had refused to take any of the spoils offered him by the King of Sodom, God said, *I will make your reward very great* (*Genesis* 15:1).

Abram, however, responded, *What good will your gifts be if I keep on being childless?* His wife Sarai was barren. Abram had waited a year, then five years, ten years, fifteen years—no child! Abram got worried so he adopted his servant Eliezar as his heir. God, however, vetoed his choice, *No, that one shall not be your heir; your own issue shall be your heir* (*Genesis* 15:4).

Then God led Abram out into the night and said, *Look up at the sky and count the stars. Just so shall your descendants be.* Though he and Sarai were aged, Abram believed. Then God went one step further. The great reward He promised him was to be not only an heir, but an inheritance as well—*This land* (*Genesis* 15:7).

As proof of these promises God made a convenant with Abram. Covenant comes from the word "cut"; for covenants were ratified by cutting animals in two and the parties to the covenant walking between the split animals as if to say, "If I break the covenant, you may cut me in two like these animals." Then the animals were roasted and a banquet sealed the covenant.

A covenant with God, however, is a contract of adherence, a unilateral pact. One party stipulates the terms, the other party is free only to adhere to them or reject them. An alien, for instance, comes to the United States. He decides he wants to be an American citizen. Uncle Sam says, "All right, but you must agree to these terms." Uncle Sam stipulates the terms, and the alien is free to accept or reject them.

In a covenant with man, God stipulates the terms and man is only free to adhere to them. That is why in making the covenant with Abram a flaming torch, symbol of God, passes between the split pieces. For it is only God who sets the terms: promises an heir and an inheritance to Abram—*this land.* God further tells Abram that the land would be given to his descendants only after much suffering: *Your descendants shall be aliens in a land not their own, where they shall be enslaved and oppressed for four hundred years . . . . But I will bring judgment on the nation they must serve, and in the end they will depart with great wealth. You, however, shall join your forefathers in peace; you shall be buried at a contented old age (Genesis* 15:13-15).

After God had made these promises of land and descendants to Abram, ten years passed. Abram was eighty-five years old, and Sarai seventy-five. So both she and Abram panicked. They lost patience. It's so hard to wait for God. So they took things into their own hands to fulfill God's word. Sarai gave Abram her handmaiden, the Egyptian Hagar. In those days, substitute motherhood was customary in cases of sterility. It demonstrates the great desire of Semitic women to have children—even by proxy.

However, as always happens when we take things into our own hands, the outcome of this solution was anything but happy. When Hagar conceived and brought forth a son, named Ishmael, she disdained Sarai. Sarai in turn so abused Hagar that she fled from her mistress. But an angel of the Lord told Hagar to return to her mistress. She did and submitted to Sarai for thirteen years. God comforted Hagar by telling her that the descendants of her son Ishmael would be too many to count. How good and loving is God; He cares for even a despised and rejected foreign slave.

As if God were angry at Abram for having listened to Sarai and taking Hagar to wife, God did not speak to Abram for thirteen years. Finally, when Abram was ninety-nine years old, physically unable to have a child, and when Abram was beginning to pin all his hopes on thirteen-year-old Ishmael, the Lord appeared to Abram and personalized the covenant He had already made with him. God laid down two conditions: first, *walk before Me and be perfect*—that is, be completely dedicated to me so that I may bless you; and secondly, accept only me *(El Shaddai)* as God.

Then God reaffirmed Abram's destiny by changing his name to Abraham meaning "father of a host of nations." For their part, Abraham and his descendants were to show their acceptance of the covenant by circumcision. Circumcision existed before this event. It used to be a rite of kinship, made at puberty. Now God made it a religious rite—a symbol of kinship with Himself, to be made at infancy, eight days after a child's birth.

Then God told Abraham to change Sarai's name to Sarah, and He promised to give her a son. Abraham laughed, but not in a sneer of unbelief, but in awe and wonderment. Abraham was a man of faith, but still a man. His faith was not perfect. He accepted the substance of God's promises, but questioned the details. Both he and Sarah were old, way beyond the age of childbearing. Moreover, he had come to love Ishmael and was perfectly content to have him as his heir. So he begged God, *Let but Ishmael live on in your favor (Genesis* 17:8). God turned down Abraham's plea and repeated that Sarah would have a son, and you shall call him Isaac. With wonderful obedience, Abraham accepted both God's covenant and His promise of a son by having his entire household circumcised.

Shortly afterwards, three visitors came to Abraham at Mamre, near present-day Hebron. Abraham's generous hospitality merited a great reward. The three visitors were probably Yahweh and two angels. The posterity of Abraham was so important in Salvation History that Yahweh himself came to announce that Sarah would have a son within a year. Sarah, who was perhaps eavesdropping, laughed at the prediction, for she was so old. However, her laugh too was not a sneer; rather it was a play on words: in Hebrew the words "laugh" and "Isaac" sound alike. The birth of a son to a couple so old prepared God's people to accept the virgin birth of the Messiah.

When the three visitors departed, they headed toward Sodom. Abraham accompanied them to see them on their way. It was then the Yahweh told Abraham, as a friend, that He planned to destroy Sodom. He allowed Abraham to behold this judgment of God so that he might teach his children to shun evil and walk in the way of goodness.

However, Lot lived in Sodom. So Abraham protested, *Will you sweep away the innocent with the guilty?* (*Genesis* 18:23). So, relying on the prerogative of a friend, Abraham bargained with God. The scene was much like one that occurred daily in the bazaars of the East. *Would you wipe out the city if there were fifty innocent people?* Abraham asked God. Then he pares it down to forty-five, forty, thirty, twenty. Abraham ceased bargaining when he reached the irreducible minimum of ten! What charity Abraham exemplified to be so concerned about others. Also, a few good people, like lightning rods, can prevent the lightning bolts of God's punishment from striking the wicked.

Not ten good people could be found, so the two angels,

not Yahweh, continued on to Sodom and reached the city in the evening. Lot extended hospitality to them. But in the evening the townsmen of Sodom surrounded Lot's house to abuse sexually his two visitors—an ample illustration of the thorough rottenness of these people. Lot offered them his two virginal daughters in lieu of the two visitors—a surprising action. It seemed to Lot that hospitality took precedence over the virginal honor of his own daughters. In response to Lot's offer, these perverts threatened to molest Lot himself.

Fortunately for Lot, his visitors rescued him. Forcibly, they led Lot, his wife and two daughters to safety outside the city. To explain the human-like form of a salt rock formation near the Dead Sea, the story was told that Lot's wife looked back upon the perishing cities and was turned into a pillar of salt. Her backward glance revealed her heart was still in Sodom; she preferred the pleasures of Sodom to obedience to God's command. *Who seeks his life shall lose it* (*Luke* 17:32-3).

Lot and his two daughters fled to Zoar and out of consideration for Lot, Zoar was not destroyed. At sunrise sulphurous fire rained down upon Sodom and Gomorrah and the cities of the Plain. The destruction of the cities was probably due to an earthquake: fissures in the earth that released sulphurous gases (brimstone) which became ignited and caused a great holocaust. The next morning Abraham looked toward Sodom and Gomorrah and saw dense smoke over the land rising like fumes from a furnace.

Poor Lot. His story is a perennial warning against compromise. Lot's primary concern was for the temporal, not for the spiritual. He chose the rich lands of Sodom and the Plains. He yielded to a spirit of worldliness and mingled with the godless Sodomites for worldly advantage. His end was miserable. He ended up cowering in a cave, penniless, stripped of all his earthly possessions; his wife had turned into a pillar of salt; his sons-in-law had been destroyed in Sodom; and Lot himself had to live with the fruits of the sin of incest, for his two daughters had tricked him into fathering two sons: Moab and Ammon, the ancestors of the despised Moabites and Ammonites. Yet through all this, Lot remained a just man (*1 Peter* 2:7-8).

Abraham at Gerar (Chapter 20). After having viewed the terrible destruction of Sodom, Abraham journeyed from Mamre to Gerar, about thirty miles west of Beersheba. The incident with Abimelech very likely combines elements found in two very similar but distinct stories in *Genesis* 12:10-20 and 26:6-11. The story is put here to show how God safeguarded the promise He had made to Abraham, despite Abraham's fear for his life. Also, it shows that God holds all men to the moral law, even pagans.

Chapter 6

The Isaac Story

The birth and circumcision of Isaac (Chapter 21).
God takes His time. He waited twenty-five years before
empowering Sarah to give birth to Isaac. He waited until it
was humanly impossible for Abraham to have a child; he
was one hundred years old. Isaac's birth at this time in
Abraham's life showed very clearly that his birth was the
fruit of God's action. It typified the virginal birth of Jesus.

After Isaac's birth, Hagar was dismissed from Abraham's
household at Sarah's insistence. Sarah wanted to make sure
her son Isaac, not Ishmael, would be Abraham's heir. Hagar
with Ishmael headed back home toward Egypt through the
wilderness of Paran. There, Ishmael became a great hunter
and married an Egyptian girl. His descendants became the
Arabs of Paran, blessed by God because of Abraham.

At this time, Abraham made a covenant with Abimelech—
a non-aggression pact. To ratify the covenant Abraham gave
Abimelech seven ewe lambs. The place was called Beersheba (well of the seven sheep). Abraham dwelled there for
many years.

The testing of Abraham (Chapter 22). Abraham's life
reached its climax in the supreme test given him by God.
God said to him, *Take your only son Isaac whom you love
and offer him up as a holocaust to me.* What a test! He was
to sacrifice his only son—the one he loved! God's command
must have been given in a night vision, for *early in the
morning* Abraham did what God had bidden him. What
great faith Abraham had! He complied with God's wishes
because he believed that God could raise up Isaac even from

the dead (*Hebrews* 11:17-19).

Later tradition states that Abraham went to Mt. Moriah, the hill on which Solomon would later build his Temple. On the way, we are told that Isaac carried the wood for the sacrifice. With the naive simplicity of a child, Isaac asked, *Father! We have the fire and the wood but where is the sheep for the holocaust?* Abraham, *hoping against hope* (*Romans* 4:18), answered, *God will provide* (the Motto of Rhode Island). Then the two continued on in the oppressive silence of the father who knows.

On the mount, Abraham built an altar, arranged the wood, bound Isaac and laid him on the wood. God tests his own to the last extremity, for only after Abraham had reached out and took the knife to slay Isaac did God intervene and forbid the sacrifice. By this act, God condemned the Canaanite practice of child sacrifice.

The sacrifice of Isaac is the only hint in the Old Testament that God would demand human sacrifice to redeem the human race. And the fact that God did what He had prevented Abraham from doing, namely, He sacrificed His Son—His only One, the One whom He loves, *my beloved Son*—reveals the incredible depth of His love for us.

The two servants whom Abraham brought along for the sacrifice typified the two thieves who accompanied Jesus to Calvary. Isaac carried the wood for his sacrifice, Jesus carried the cross to Calvary. It took three days to reach the hill of sacrifice, during that time Isaac was as good as dead. Jesus lay in the tomb for three days.

Abraham's faith was tested four times. The test consisted in giving up something or someone especially dear to himself. First, He was asked to leave his homeland and kinsfolk; then to separate from Lot; then to give up Ishmael; and lastly, to sacrifice his only son Isaac.

The life of a Christian is but a series of tests, for that is how character is built. God starts with little demands, then

He follows up with greater and greater ones, just as examinations get harder and harder the further we progress in education. The most terrible test God put Abraham to was that he sacrifice the love of his life, Isaac, and to do this by his own hand! Yet Abraham responded promptly. He had learned that God is to be trusted! *God will provide!* And He did!

The death and burial of Sarah (Chapter 23). When Sarah was one hundred twenty-seven years old, she died in Hebron. Did the terrible ordeal of sacrificing Isaac hasten her death? Abraham bought the cave of Machpelah in which to bury her. He paid an exorbitant price for it. But it mattered not to Abraham; in his piety he would have nothing but the most decent burial site for his beloved wife. The purchase of this land, though small, was a foothold; it gave Abraham's descendants their first land rights in the Promised Land. Today the cave of Machpelah is covered by a large mosque. And there Abraham is honored by Muslims, Christians, and Jews, followers of the three great monotheistic religions of the world.

Isaac and Rebecca (Chapter 24). Abraham now had one last duty to perform: to find a wife for Isaac. So he sent his old servant, perhaps Eliezer of Genesis 15:2, back to Haran, the city of his brother Nahor. Abraham did not want Isaac to marry a Canaanite woman lest he be led to infidelity to the one God. In Haran Abraham's brother Nahor had a son Bathuel. Bathuel had two children: Laban and Rebekah (*Genesis* 22:23).

God was with Eliezer. God prospers those who trust in Him. His sending Rebekah to Eliezer is one of the most charming stories in Genesis. When Isaac saw Rebekah he fell deeply in love with her, for Rebekah was both beautiful and clever. Isaac's love for her comforted him after the death of his mother Sarah (*Genesis* 24:67).

Abraham took another wife, after Sarah's death. Her name was Keturah. Through her Abraham became the ancestor of many Arab tribes (*Genesis* 25:1-4). To these sons of his concubine, Abraham gave substantial gifts and sent them away so that Isaac might be totally free to fulfill the promises of the Lord in the land of Canaan.

At the ripe old age of one hundred seventy-five Abraham died. Both Isaac and Ishmael buried him in the cave of Machpelah near Hebron beside his wife Sarah.

Chapter 7

The Jacob Story
(Chapter 25)

Isaac was around forty years old when he married Rebekah (*Genesis* 25:20). Rebekah was sterile, so Isaac prayed for her. Twenty years later, God heard his prayer, and Rebekah bore twins: Esau and Jacob. They were totally different.

Esau was red and hairy. When he grew up, he became a skillful hunter. But like that other hunter Nimrod, he too became a rebel (*Genesis* 10:8 ff.). Isaac preferred him to Jacob, because Isaac was fond of game. Esau was an outdoorsman. His descendants were the Edomites; thus he came to typify unbelievers.

Jacob, on the contrary, was a homebody, *who kept to his tents*. He typified the believers—the Israelites. Rebekah preferred Jacob to Esau.

One day Jacob was cooking a stew. Esau came in from the open field famished. He said to Jacob, *Let me gulp down some of that red stuff. I'm starving*. Esau didn't even know what Jacob was cooking. He didn't care. Like an animal, he wanted to "gulp" down whatever it was.

Jacob, however, shrewdly replied, *Give me your birthright in exchange*. To sell one's birthright was legal but incredible in the eyes of the Israelites. The birthright was one's most cherished possession in those days. It entitled the first-born to a double share of the father's inheritance; made one head of the family; and the one responsible for carrying on the family name. Esau displayed his stupidity and lack of spiritual awareness by having no appreciation for these things. *I'm going to die one day,* said Esau, *so what good will my birthright do me? I can't live on promises. Give me something to eat—tomorrow I die.* So for a mess of pottage, Esau sold his birthright to Jacob.

The significance of this event in the infancy narrative of Jesus' life is often overlooked. King Herod was an Edomite, a descendant of Esau. As such, he knew he had no right to the throne of Israel. For this reason Herod in a jealous rage ordered all male children, two years or under, in Bethlehem to be slain. In this way Herod hoped to destroy the rightful king of the Jews coming from the line of Jacob.

Not only did Esau ignore his birthright, but he seemed to have no scruples about marrying Canaanite women against the will of his father and mother. When about forty, he married two Hittite women to the great sorrow of his parents.

Even though these actions of Esau cooled Isaac's favor toward him, Isaac felt as he approached death that he must bless his oldest son. So he told Esau to prepare for him his favorite dish of food from the chase.

Rebekah overheard Isaac's request and plotted to secure Isaac's blessing for Jacob. Jacob concurred with her. He lied to Isaac and secured his blessing. How often God chooses weak and little things, like Rebekah and Jacob, to fulfill His plan of Salvation History. However, their sins did not go unpunished. Rebekah was punished by becoming separated from Jacob all the rest of her life. Jacob, in turn, was punished when Laban deceived him about Rachel and when his own sons later lied to him about Joseph—both deceptions caused Jacob years of unspeakable anguish.

When Isaac discovered what Jacob had done, he was seized with *a fit of uncontrollable trembling* (*Genesis* 27:33). He realized he had been going against God's will in preferring Esau. So he yielded to God's will and sent Jacob to Haran to prevent his marrying Canaanite women and to protect him against the wrath of Esau.

How many of us, like Esau, sell our birthright for a mess of pottage. One thing Our Lady lamented in this our day was the great apostasy of so many from the Catholic faith.

> At the devil's booth are all things sold,
> Each ounce of dross costs its ounce of gold;
> For a cap and bells our lives we pay,
> Bubbles we buy with a whole soul's tasking;
> 'Tis Heaven alone that is given away,
> 'Tis only God may be had for the asking; . . .
> (Lowell's *The Vision of Sir Launfal.*)

How many, like Rebekah and Jacob, do evil to draw good from it. Yet God is not mocked: both Rebekah and Jacob paid the price for their iniquity.

Rebekah lost Jacob, for he left Beersheba and headed toward Haran. On the way he stopped at Luz. Using a stone as a pillow, he went to sleep. In his sleep he dreamt of a stairway going up from earth to Heaven with angels ascending and descending. It revealed to Jacob the traffic that goes on between Heaven and earth and that God is accessible to all who aspire to Him. Then God stood beside Jacob and promised to give him and his descendants the land whereon he slept; and He promised to multiply his descendants like the dust of the earth. In addition, God said, *I will protect you wherever you go, and bring you back to this land* (*Genesis* 28:15).

When Jacob awoke, he cried out, *How awesome is this shrine! God is here. It is the gateway to Heaven!* Jacob marked the spot with a stone monument and named the place "Bethel"—"House of God."

Though Jacob had been the recipient of so many of God's graces, still he bargained with God. *If you remain with me, if you protect me on this journey, if I come back safe, you shall be my God and I'll give back to you a tenth of all you give me.* If, if, if . . . how imperfect Jacob was at this time of his life. There is hope for all of us.

After his dream, Jacob resumed his journey. All seemed so easy now that the Lord was with him. A heart lifted up lifts up the feet! When he arrived at Haran, Jacob stopped at a well in the open country to assess things. He inquired about Laban from shepherds who were bringing their sheep to the well. At that moment Rachel, Laban's sister, came to the well with a flock of sheep.

Everything fell into place, because God was with Jacob. Covering the well was a huge stone that ordinarily only many shepherds could remove. Jacob manifested his strength by removing the stone single-handedly so that Rachel could water her sheep. Next, Jacob revealed himself to Rachel and bestowed rich gifts upon her. Rachel ran home to tell her brother Laban the news, and Laban rushed out to meet Jacob and bring him to his house.

In Laban's treatment of Jacob, we see God's justice at work; namely, the Law of Retribution: the deceiver is deceived. Jacob worked seven years for the hand of Rachel. Instead, on his wedding night he was given not the beautiful Rachel but the not so beautiful Leah. Such a deception was possible because a woman was veiled before marriage. In this indirect way, Jacob was taught to respect the rights of the first-born.

When Jacob discovered the deception, Laban offered him Rachel on the condition that he work seven more years for her hand. After the wedding ceremony of Leah, a seven-day affair, Jacob married Rachel and he loved her more than Leah.

After this double marriage, there followed what seemed like a rapid-fire birth race. Leah had six sons and a daughter: Reuben, Simeon, Levi, Judah, Issachar, Zebulun and Dinah. Two more sons were born to Jacob through

Leah's maidservant Zilpah: Gad and Asher. Rachel gave Jacob two sons: Joseph and Benjamin. Her maidservant Bilhah gave him two more: Dan and Naphtali (*Genesis* 35:22-26). Jacob's twelve sons became the ancestors of the twelve tribes of Israel. That was why each birth was noted separately.

The evils of bigamy surfaced in Jacob's family life. Family peace and harmony were shattered by internal strife and factions. Sons born of a common mother, such as Joseph and Benjamin, clung together; whereas, later on, Leah's sons plot to kill their half brother Joseph.

Jacob outwits Laban (Chapter 30). After Rachel had given birth to Joseph, Jacob wished to return home. He was homesick—he had been in Haran twenty-one years; and Laban's attitude toward him had changed. Moreover, God had told him to *return to the land of your fathers* (*Genesis* 31:31).

But Jacob did not want to go home empty-handed, so he made a deal with Laban. In the Near East, sheep are white and goats are generally black. Jacob agreed to take as his wages only off-colored stock: dark sheep and speckled goats. Since few of these were normally expected, Laban seemed to be getting a great bargain. But Jacob was clever and knew more about breeding than the average shepherds or goatherds. He soon increased the odd-colored flock and grew increasingly prosperous.

Jacob leaves Haran (Chapter 31). Sufficiently wealthy now, Jacob fled from Haran in secret. When Laban learned of his flight, he pursued Jacob in anger. But God keeps His words; He watches over His own. He had promised Jacob, *I will protect you* (*Genesis* 28:15). So in a dream God warned Laban not to harm Jacob. Thus when Laban overtook Jacob in Gilead, he simply rebuked him severely for leaving the way he did.

After Laban bade his daughters farewell and departed for Haran, Jacob proceeded on his way and was met by a host of angels. They formed two armies or camps standing on each side of Jacob to protect him. So Jacob called the place Mahanaim, "two camps." God was assuring Jacob at this critical moment, as he entered the Promised Land and prepared to meet his brother Esau, of His continued presence and protection.

Despite these assurances, Jacob was still apprehensive about Esau. When he had left Canaan, Esau was on the verge of killing him. So with his usual cleverness and tact, Jacob sent out feelers to find out if Esau were still angry with him. He learned that Esau was living in Seir in the country of Edom and was coming with four hundred men to meet him.

This news greatly distressed Jacob. So he divided his company into two groups, reasoning that if Esau destroyed one, the other could escape. Then he prayed to God for deliverance. *Save me, Lord,* he prayed *from the hand of Esau (Genesis* 32:12).

After his prayer, Jacob made last-minute preparations to meet Esau. He sent large numbers of animals from his herds as a present to Esau. He sent them in successive droves. He hoped the rich gifts would appease his brother and make it clear that Jacob had no need to demand his birthright, because he was already rich. As a final precaution, he sent his family and flocks across the Jabbok River at night while he stayed behind alone.

That night God sent an angel to wrestle with Jacob. The "man" (an angel in human form) wrestled with Jacob because he wanted Jacob to acknowledge his own nothingness and to begin putting all his trust in the Lord. Up to this point, Jacob was the "heel-grabber"—always doing things on his own, always trusting his own wisdom and resourcefulness. The struggle lasted the whole night. So at daybreak the "man" struck Jacob's hip and wrenched it from it's socket to teach him of his own helplessness and to move him to cling to the Lord. Jacob learned the lesson because he would not let the angel go until the angel blessed him.

This whole incident was meant to point out that when Jacob returned to Canaan, he was a changed man. His twenty-one years of experience with God at Haran had changed him from a man ambitious for self to one focused solely on doing God's will. To signify this conversion, the angel changed Jacob's name to Israel. Israel meant *one who had struggled with God and men and had prevailed* (*Genesis* 32:29).

Jacob meets Esau (Chapter 33). When Jacob meets Esau, he says, *To come into your presence is for me like coming into the presence of God* (*Genesis* 33:10). Perhaps that was the way Jacob felt when he met Esau, surrounded by four hundred men. Despite all his trepidations, Jacob was treated kindly and with love by Esau. No doubt Isaac had warned Esau to treat Jacob kindly; but ultimately it was God who touched the heart of Esau, as He had Laban's.

A bit of Esau's greed showed when he asked about the droves of cattle sent to him. He half hoped they were for him. When he learned they were, he took them and departed.

Was not this meeting between Jacob and Esau strange? After twenty years of separation, you would think there would be feasting and banqueting. But no, everything was matter of fact, cool, and brief.

Perhaps Jacob still didn't trust Esau. He seemed to want to get away from him as soon as possible. He even lied, so it seems. Esau wanted Jacob to follow him to Seir. Jacob made excuses. He told Esau he would meet him in Seir, then Jacob headed in the opposite direction to Succoth and encamped there in the sight of Shechem. Jacob bought the land, pitched his tents there, and built an altar to the God of Israel. This land purchase was historically important, for the bones of Joseph would be buried there (*Joshua* 24:32). Here also was the well of Jacob where Jesus conversed with the Samaritan woman (*John* 4:6).

The Rape of Dinah (Chapter 34). Jacob dwelt at Succoth for seven years. During that time, Dinah, daughter of Leah, was raped by Shechem. Her two brothers, Simeon and Levi, slaughtered the Shechemites in revenge. Jacob weakly reprimanded them and was worried, not knowing which way to turn. *You have brought trouble upon me*, he told Simeon and Levi. *If the inhabitants of the land unite against me and attack me, I and my family will be wiped out.*

But once again, God stepped in to save Jacob. *Go to Bethel,* He told him. *Settle there and build an altar to me.* So Jacob ordered all his family to get rid of their foreign gods and to turn to the God who had always been with him in his hour of need. They did. And immediately God saved Jacob from the vengeance of the inhabitants of the land. *As they set out for Bethel, the terror of God fell upon the towns round about, so that no one pursued the sons of Jacob* (*Genesis* 35:5).

At Bethel, God appeared to Jacob, changed his name to Israel, renewed His promise to multiply his descendants and to give this land promised to Abraham and Isaac to him. Jacob erected a pillar of stone here and called the place Bethel.

At this point we are told of the death of Rebekah's nurse, Deborah. Very likely, Deborah was with Jacob because Rebekah on her death bed must have sent her to take care of her son, Jacob. How Rebekah must have loved Jacob to send him her nurse!

From Bethel, Jacob journeyed to Bethlehem. Perhaps he heard that his father Isaac was near death. On the way Rachel bore him a second son. Rachel desired to call him Ben-oni "son of my sorrow." But Jacob refused to let him carry so unlucky a name through life and so he renamed him Benjamin, "son of my right hand." Rachel died and was buried north of Bethlehem. Jacob went on toward Mamre. On the way Ruben, his firstborn son, went and lay with Bilhah, Rachel's maid and Jacob's concubine. Jacob was deeply offended at this.

Finally, Jacob arrived at Mamre and Isaac died at the age of one hundred eighty years. Both Jacob and Esau buried him. After giving genealogical lists of the descendants of Esau, the father of the Edomites, Esau passed out of the picture.

Chapter 8

The Joseph Story
(Chapter 37)

How patient God was with Jacob. In early and middle life, Jacob walked in the energy of the flesh. He relied on his cleverness, his own strength, and his resourcefulness. But toward the end of his life, grace triumphed—and it did so through the cross.

What pain it must have been for Jacob not to have been at the bedside of his dearly beloved mother Rebekah when she died. How devastating was Rachel's death to him. When Reuben, his oldest son, defiled his concubine Bilhah, Jacob was crushed. Then no sooner did he arrive home and his father Isaac died. Yet a still heavier cross awaited Jacob: the loss of his most beloved son Joseph.

Whom God loves He chastises, not to punish, but to purify. Afflictions are love-gifts. God permits them to bless us—"sweet are the uses of adversity," to wean us from the things of earth, and to get us to surrender to the Lord, to cast all our cares on Him.

The evils of polygamy again surfaced in Joseph's unhappy relations with his half brothers. One cause for their hating him was that Joseph naively tattle-taled on the foul conduct of Dan, Naphtali, Gad and Asher. Then Jacob himself, usually so wise, unwisely gave preferential treatment to Joseph, because he was the child of his old age and of his best loved wife Rachel. Blind to Joseph's danger and the undercurrent of human passions right under his nose, Jacob showed his preference for Joseph by making him a fine tunic. Finally, Joseph once again fanned the flames of envy still more by imprudently—he was only seventeen—

relating two dreams in which he was given preference over his father and brothers.

After all this, Jacob one day sent Joseph to see how his brothers were doing. They were pasturing their father's flocks around Shechem. Jacob feared for them lest the neighboring peoples attack them in retaliation for his sons' slaughter of the Shechemites over the rape of Dinah. When Joseph arrived at Shechem, he discovered that his brothers had moved north to Dan. Instead of returning home, he set out to find them, so obedient was he to his father's will.

When his brothers saw him coming, they saw a chance to rid themselves of Joseph. One account credits Reuben with trying to save Joseph's life by having him cast into a dry cistern. Another account credits Judah with saving his life by suggesting that Joseph be sold as a slave to some Midianites. Whichever is true, they soaked Joseph's tunic with blood, and Jacob seeing it believed a wild animal had killed his son. His grief knew no bounds. How dearly Israel paid for once having deceived his own father Isaac!

Joseph's story is interrupted here by the story of Judah (Chapter 38). Perhaps it was put here because of the importance of Judah and Thamar as ancestors of the Messiah (*Matthew* 1:13). Also, Judah's immorality highlights Joseph's virtue when he was tempted to adultery.

In Egypt Joseph was sold to Potiphar, Pharaoh's chief steward. Joseph rose quickly to power. He was a fine appearing and trustworthy lad. Then too the Lord was with him and made Potiphar's household prosper under Joseph as never before.

The trial to which Joseph was subjected by Potiphar's lecherous wife confirmed his sterling character. When she tempted him to impurity, Joseph did what everyone should do when tempted against purity—he fled! Scupoli in his classic book *The Spiritual Combat* always advises us to fight sin head on; the only time he counsels retreat is when we are tempted to impurity—"Once more I say to thee, Fly! for thou art as stubble . . . trust not your strong resolutions . . . the strongest steel will melt in fire" (p.53). Joseph fled, even though it meant imprisonment or possibly death.

Once more Joseph was wronged for striving to be good. Thrown into prison, he gained the confidence of the head jailor and was entrusted with his affairs, which again prospered under him. At the same time Pharaoh's baker and cup-bearer, the two in charge of his food and drink, were also imprisoned. In jail, Joseph correctly interpreted their dreams: the cup-bearer would be restored to office, the baker would be hanged. It so happened. Yet the cup-bearer forgot all about Joseph.

Joseph typifies the life of Jesus in many ways. Joseph became a slave in Egypt; the Son of God emptied Himself and took the form of a slave. Joseph brought blessings to Egypt; Jesus blessed the world. Joseph was tempted; so was Jesus. Joseph was falsely accused before Potiphar; so was Jesus before Pilate. Joseph won the respect of his jailor; Jesus won the heart of the centurion who crucified Him. In prison Joseph was with two criminals, Pharaoh's cup-bearer and baker; on the cross Jesus hung between two thieves. Joseph told the cup-bearer he would be restored to office; Jesus promised the good thief he would that day be in paradise. Joseph was buried in a dungeon; Jesus, in a tomb—both arose to a new and better life.

Though Pharaoh's cup-bearer forgot Joseph, God did not. In fact He used the Pharaoh to release him. Dreams continued to play a part in Joseph's life. God sent Pharaoh a two-part dream about cows and ears of grain that defied the wisdom of all the wizards and magicians of Egypt. At this impasse, the cup-bearer remembered Joseph.

Joseph was summoned from prison and interpreted the Pharaoh's dream. The cows reflected Isis, the goddess of fertility; seven symbolized completeness or fullness. The seven cows and the seven ears of grain Joseph told Pharaoh both signified the same thing; namely that there were going to be in Egypt seven years of plenty and seven years of famine. Then he advised Pharaoh what he had to do.

God was warning Pharaoh to prepare for famine. Pharaoh could have laughed at Joseph. But he believed. He made Joseph second only to himself; gave him Asenath, the daughter of Potiphera, who was a priest of Heliopolis. During the years of plenty, Joseph had two sons by Asenath: Manasses and Ephraim. Joseph was 30 years old at the time. It was about 1650 B.C.

Joseph could probably never have risen to such high power in Egypt were it not for the fact that the Hyksos, or Shepherd-Kings, had usurped the Egyptian throne around 1710-1567 B.C. The Hyksos were foreigners, probably of Semitic stock, like Joseph. They probably introduced the chariot into Egypt.

Sorrow may endure for a night, but joy comes in the morning. Better the end of a thing, than the beginning. So it was with Joseph. All is well that ends well. And it does end well for those who trust in God, as Joseph did.

The famine spread to the land of Canaan and brought the sons of Jacob to Joseph. As Joseph had dreamt back home, his brothers now prostrated themselves before him in quest of food. Joseph recognized them, but they did not recognize Joseph. Joseph was desirous to see if they had changed and repented of their evil deed against himself. So at first he treated them roughly. The cross brings sinners to repentance. Thus when he imprisoned Simeon, Joseph heard them say, *We are being punished because of our brother. We saw the anguish of his heart when he pleaded with us yet we paid no heed . . .* (*Genesis* 42:21). Their consciences still bothered them.

Joseph sent them home ladened with corn, but he ordered his servants to put the money they had paid for the corn back into their sacks. That night when they discovered the money, they became afraid again. They asked each other, *What is this that God had done to us?*

When all their corn was used up, they returned a second time to Egypt—but with double money. Joseph was still not sure that his brothers had changed so he planted his drinking cup in Benjamin's sack. His threat to keep Benjamin extracted from Judah the confession Joseph was waiting for. Judah's confession revealed that he and his brothers had changed and were sorry for the past wrongs they had done to their father Jacob. They did not want to repeat an act that would kill him. This is the climax of the Joseph story. As soon as Joseph learned that his brothers had changed, he revealed himself to them.

Naturally, they were fearful. Would he now avenge himself on them. Joseph allayed their fears by telling them that all that happened to him was planned by God to save their lives in an extraordinary deliverance. *It was really for the sake of saving lives that God sent me here ahead of you . . . So it was not really you but God who had me come here* (*Genesis* 45:5,8). This is the key to the Joseph story: "There is a divinity that shapes our ends, rough-hew them how we will."

> My life is but a weaving
> Between my Lord and me,
> I cannot choose the colors
> He weaveth steadily.
>
> Oftimes He weaveth sorrow,
> And I in foolish pride
> Forget He sees the upper
> And I, the underside.
>
> He knows, He loves, He cares,
> Nothing this truth can dim.

He gives His very best to those
Who leave the choice with Him.

Pharaoh having heard of the visit of Joseph's brothers invited the family to come to Egypt. So high was his regard for Joseph that he offered them the land of Goshen, the fat of the land, an ideal place for settlement. Also, it was close to where Joseph lived, for the Hyksos had moved the capital of Egypt to the Delta area.

The Pharaoh, moreover, ordered that wagons be sent to Jacob to transport the women and children on the long journey from Canaan to Egypt. The joy of Jacob, upon learning of Joseph's safety and high position, defies description. Jacob cared nothing for Joseph's high position. *It is enough,* he exclaimed *that he is still alive (Genesis* 45:28).

Jacob immediately set out from Hebron to Egypt. But at Beersheba, the sanctuary close to Isaac, Jacob offered sacrifice to God. He wondered what God thought of his leaving the Promised Land. God had told Isaac not to go to Egypt (*Genesis* 26:2). Was God of the same mind still? God assured Jacob that it was all right for him to migrate to Egypt at this time, and He promised to bring him back after the death of Joseph. Assured of God's help, Jacob went down to Egypt with his whole family: *seventy persons in all* (*Genesis* 46:30).

When Judah announced to Joseph that Jacob was coming, Joseph mounted a chariot to meet his father. The meeting was too emotional for words. Joseph flung himself on Jacob's neck *and wept a long time in his arms* (*Genesis* 46:29).

Next Joseph introduced five of his brothers to Pharaoh. Then when he brought his father, Pharaoh asked Jacob how old he was. Jacob answered, *One hundred and thirty years; few and hard have been these years of my life* (*Genesis* 47:9). Few years compared with Abraham who lived one hundred seventy-five years and Isaac who died when one hundred eighty years old; and hard years, separated as Jacob had been from his dear mother Rebekah for twenty-one years and living all those years in dread of Esau.

During the years of famine Joseph introduced a harsh land program. First, he took the people's money for food, then their cattle, then their land; as a result the government owned the land and a return of twenty percent of the produce of the land went to Pharaoh. After their bitter experience with the Egyptians during the time of the Exodus, Israel rejoiced that Joseph had reduced the Egyptians almost to slavery. In their eyes, his harshness was just one more jewel in his crown.

Jacob lived in Egypt seventeen years; his life span was one hundred forty-seven years. When the time came for him to die, he summoned Joseph and made him promise that he would not bury him in Egypt, the land of darkness and unbelief. Sometime later, he adopted Joseph's two sons: Ephraim and Manasseh. After that, Israel on his deathbed called his sons to gather around him that he might tell them what was to happen to them and their descendants in the days to come.

He addressed first the six sons of Leah. Reuben the firstborn would be deprived of his rights as firstborn because he had defiled his father's bed. His tribe would decrease and dwell on the east of the Jordan in the lowest place. In the history of Israel the tribe of Reuben was a nonentity—from it came no judge, no prophet, no king. How terrible are the wages of sin!

Simeon and Levi because of their cruelty toward the Shechemites were promised nothing of value. Levi would be scattered throughout Israel and Simeon would be practically absorbed by Judah. Since Joseph in Egypt held Simeon hostage, it probably was Simeon who had concocted the conspiracy to get rid of Joseph.

Jacob compared Judah to a lion at rest after a successful hunt. He would rule Israel. Only when his rule would pass out of his hands would the Messiah come. This happened when the Jews rejected Jesus before Pilate.

Zebulun would dwell by the sea and become a commercial sea-faring people.

Isaachar would be likened to a strong ass. In those days the ass was an honorable beast. His descendants would be farmers, not shepherds, enslaved by their Canaanite overlords.

Next Jacob addressed the sons of his concubines.

Bilhah's sons: Dan and Naphtali. Dan would free his people. Samson was a Danite. Yet he would be a viper. Judas was from the tribe of Dan. In the book of Revelation this tribe is omitted, because it was believed that the Anti-Christ would spring from the tribe of Dan.

Naphtali—Barak who defeated Sisera was from this tribe (*Judges* 4). The cities of Capernaum, Bethsaida, and Chorazin were in the region of Naphtali.

Zilpah's sons: Gad and Asher. Gad's descendants would live east of the Jordan and keep to the bedouin way of life. They would "gad about"—be a wandering tribe. Both Dan and Gad raised cattle; so they desired pastures east of the Jordan. Being on the border of Israel, they were always the first to suffer attacks from desert bands and so lived in a state of constant warfare; and they were generally the first tribes to be led into captivity.

Asher would dwell along the seacoast adjacent to the cities of Tyre and Sidon. The prophetess Anna at Jesus' Presentation was from the tribe of Asher.

Finally, Jacob addressed Rachel's two sons, Joseph and Benjamin.

Jacob asked God to bless Joseph with all kinds of fruitfulness. Actually, Joseph received a double portion, the firstborn's birthright, because his two sons Ephraim and

Manasses were numbered among the twelve tribes of Israel. Joshua was from the tribe of Joseph.

Benjamin would be like a wolf in swiftness and ferocity. Saul, Israel's first king, was from the tribe of Benjamin. Saul, the great persecutor of the early Church, who with the rapacity of a wolf seized the early Christians like sheep, was also from this tribe. Later, he would become Paul the greatest missionary in the Church, seizing souls from the wolf pack of Satan and his demons.

After his farewell address to his sons and after eliciting from them the promise that they would bury him in the land of his fathers in the field of Machpelah facing Mamre, Jacob died.

After seventy days of mourning Joseph took his father's embalmed body back to Canaan to bury him with Abraham and Sarah, Isaac and Rebekah and Leah in the cave of Machpelah.

After the burial, Joseph's brothers feared that he would now avenge himself upon them. One of the penalties of sin is to fear others are as evil as the evildoers themselves. Joseph reassured them, *Can I take the place of God? Revenge is mine,* said the Lord, *not man's.*

Joseph lived on to one hundred ten years, the perfect life span according to Egyptian standards. He reminded his brothers that God would take them out of the land to the land He had promised to Abraham, Isaac, and Jacob. Then he made them swear that when this happened, they would bring his bones with them. Moses did this. And Joshua buried the bones of Joseph in Ephraim's territory at Shechem (*Joshua* 24:32).

In the roll call of Israel's heroes of faith, this command of Joseph is singled out as the most significant act of faith in his whole life. *By faith Joseph, near the end of his life, spoke of the Exodus of the Israelites and gave instruction about his bones* (*Hebrews* 11:22).

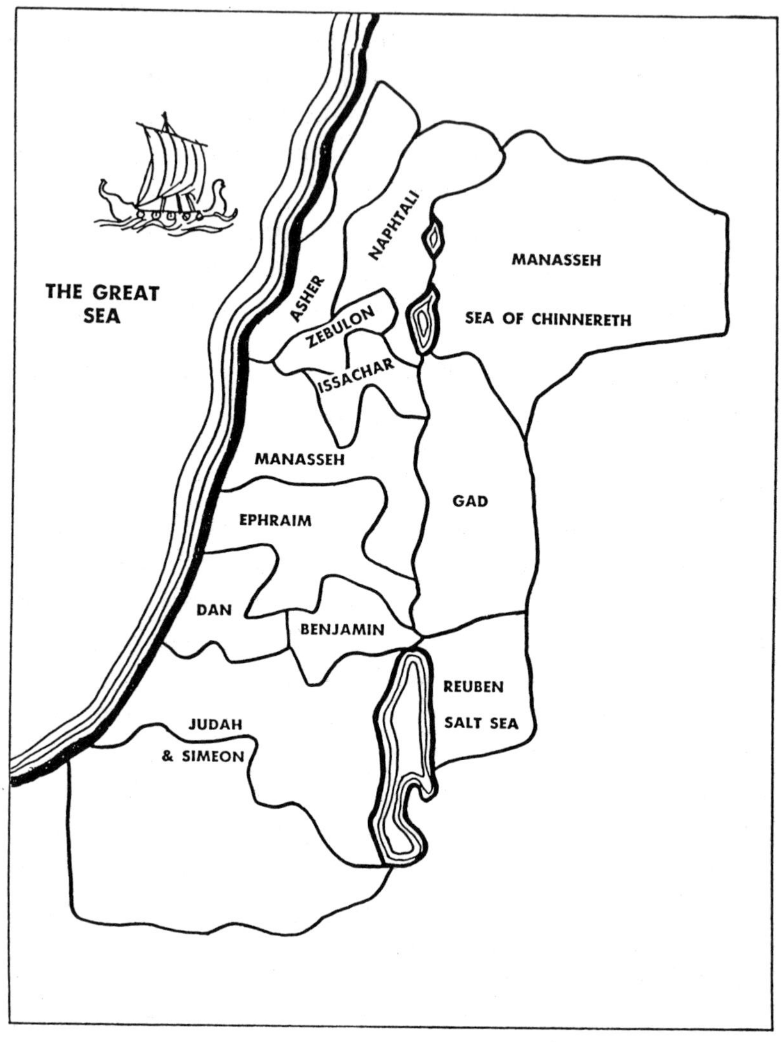
THE GREAT
SEA
ASHER
NAPHTALI
ZEBULON
ISSACHAR
MANASSEH
SEA OF CHINNERETH
MANASSEH
EPHRAIM
GAD
DAN
BENJAMIN
REUBEN
SALT SEA
JUDAH
& SIMEON

Genesis is not a book of little stories to tell children, nor is it a series of edifying incidents on which to meditate. Certainly there are lively stories and edifying passages, but these are not the point of Genesis.

The point of Genesis is to make God living and present. For so many God is an abstraction, not a personal God. Genesis gives us a living God, personal, present, and colorful.

Chapters 12 to 50 of Genesis tell us that God has a plan for humanity and the world. He called man. He chose a people: Abraham and his descendants. And He sealed His choice with a covenant. In Abraham we see faith rewarded. In Jacob we see grace as a gift freely given. In Joseph we learn that there is a divinity that shapes our ends—a Divine Providence.

Unlike paganism, God is not far away; in Genesis He is near. In paganism man seeks God; in Genesis God seeks man. In paganism the gods are indifferent to man and even cruel; in Genesis God loves man, cares for him, and desires his final good. Genesis is meant to bring us closer to God. That is how we should read it!

Appendix 1

The Pentateuch

The Pentateuch

Before Moses died (around 1250 B.C.), he left a record of the great events in which he had been privileged to play a leading part. The record consisted of historical narrative and a legal code. Some of this record was at first kept alive orally by bards and minstrels and then later some was committed to writing. This record became the substance of the Pentateuch.

The Pentateuch, like a Shakespearean drama of five acts, is a single volume composed of five books attributed to Moses: Genesis, Exodus, Leviticus, Numbers, and Deuteronomy.

Genesis explains the origins of God's people. Exodus recounts the birth of that people of God as a nation. Leviticus makes it clear this nation was to be a holy people. Numbers stresses the political side of the nation. And Deuteronomy commands that the citizens of this nation be animated with a love for God and for neighbor.

It is not possible to attribute all these books to Moses: for instance, his obituary in Deuteronomy Chapter 34.

In the beginning Israel was a pastoral people. Israel's creed began with the words, "My father was a wandering Aramean." Nomadic life was not conducive to a written literature. It was more suited to campfire songs and stories. As the clans grew, their traditions grew. Some were written down, but most of them were "talked down"—handed on by word of mouth. Thus the Psalmist wrote:

> *O God, our ears have heard,*
> *our fathers have declared to us,*
> *The deeds you did in their days*
> *in days of old* (*Psalm* 44:2).

This Oral Tradition prevailed from 1850 to 1250 B.C.

The transition from Oral Saga to Literary Epic was made during the national renaissance—the birth of the nation under the kings of Israel. This occurred about the same time that Homer was putting into writing in his *Iliad* and *Odyssey* the oral sagas of the Trojan War (940-850 B.C.).

In 1190 B.C. the Philistines had invaded the land of Canaan. They had the secret of making iron, which enabled them to dominate the land. They even named the land "Palestine"—the land of the Philistines. In 1060 B.C. they destroyed Israel's shrine at Shiloh. Israel was sorely beset. Even the mighty Samson did not prevail against the Philistines. Israel realized that to survive, it would need more than religious unity, based on a central shrine.

Their enemies had kings. So Israel begged Samuel, the last of the Judges, to give them a king and thus effect political unity. Samuel gave them Saul. But it was David, Saul's successor, who crushed the Philistines. Under him and his son Solomon, the kingdom reached its apogee. David made Jerusalem the capital of the kingdom and put the Ark of the Covenant there. Solomon built the Temple for the Ark.

With the kings, there arose a privileged class of officials: Scribes, to keep the royal archives; Priests, to serve in the Temple; Judges, to administer the law of Moses; and often Prophets, to remind the Kings of their obligations to God and the Covenant. In other words, the intellectual and cultural atmosphere of the Court favored the rise and development of literature. Peace and prosperity, however, are not only conducive to literature, but they can cause Kings to forget the spiritual destiny of their people. What was also needed was sacred literature.

So, some writers from the tribe of Judah around 970-931 B.C. gathered together the short creeds and traditions that had taken shape around the various shrines and sacred places in Israel's past. In daringly human ways, the writers spoke of God and used imagery and symbolism depicting the deepest of religious truths. Since the writers used the name Yahweh for God, their account was called the Yahwist or "J" document (the Germans used J instead of Y for Yahweh).

After Solomon's death, the kingdom was divided in 926 B.C. into North and South. Ten tribes followed Rehoboam to form the northern kingdom; and only Judah and Benjamin remained to form the southern kingdom. To prevent people from going to the Temple in Jerusalem, and thus jeopardize their allegiance, the northern kings erected their own shrines and introduced pagan practices into religion. The prophets roared in protest, but to little avail.

However, a few, under the influence of the prophets, tried to win the people back to faith in the true God by writing down the story of God's mighty deeds done in their behalf. This was about 850 to 750 B.C. These writers referred to God by the name Elohim. So their writings were called the Elohist or "E" document.

At this same time, the northern priests concerned about the lapse in morality, tried to bring Israel back to God and morality by showing them their legal roots. They wrote, in effect, that God had freely chosen them, that He had cared for them as shown by the exodus events, that He had fought for them as shown in the conquest of Canaan; therefore, their response should be—keep His Laws given to Moses. This became known as Deuteronomy or the "D" documents. Sometime during the reign of Ezechias (716-687 B.C.) the "J" and "E" documents were fused.

However, the "D" document met with a different fate. The Priests of the Temple were reluctant to accept the legal code compiled by the priests from the north, the "D" document. It was buried away in the Temple until rediscovered a century later under King Josiah (626-609 B.C.). This discovery started a reform in the nation causing the Jerusalem priests to codify their own traditions. The result was a systematic account of the origins of the religious ceremonials in Israel: the Sabbath, circumcision, Passover, Tabernacles, Priesthood, Fasts, etc., plus the Law of Holiness (*Leviticus* Chapters 17-26). This became known as the Priestly or "P" document.

The Babylonian Empire in 587 B.C. crushed Judah, its monarchy and its Temple. The Judeans were led into exile. They asked their priests and their prophets why did God permit this to happen—their God who in the past had conquered powerful Egypt and Canaan in their behalf. The priests and prophets answered, "You broke your covenant with the Lord."

The people asked, "What was the covenant?"

So the priests and the prophets gathered the exiled people together each Sabbath and began to teach them their history and the legal code which they had all but forgotten. This was the birth of the synagogue and the beginning of the editing of the Bible.

The Babylonian Captivity ended in 538 B.C. In 515 B.C. the returned exiles rebuilt the Temple of Jerusalem. The Priestly party now became the dominant power in the restored nation. It sought to rebuild the nation on the "P" document fused with the "J," "E," and "D" documents. Sometime between 500 and 400 B.C. the Pentateuch reached its final form with its two currents: History ("J" and "E") and Law ("D" and "P"). And Israel became the nation of the Book.

This documentary theory helps explain Doublets in the Pentateuch. A Doublet is two different accounts of the same event. For instance Genesis preserves two accounts of the creation, the Flood, the promise of a son to Sarah (*Genesis* 17:16-19; 18:9-15), the flight of Jacob from Canaan

(*Genesis* 27:1-46; 28:1-9). the origin of the names of Isaac, Bethel (*Genesis* 28:9; 35:15), and Israel (*Genesis* 32:28; 35:10), and the story of Joseph.

Genesis was not written all at one time by a single historian who had studied all the sources and then composed an account all his own. No, the ancient editor had too much regard for the sources to do this. If an event were recorded differently in two accounts, the editors did not pick or choose one or the other or blend them together; no, they simply put the two different accounts side by side and left it for the readers to draw their own conclusions. This method of composition explains some of the stylistic differences in Genesis and certain inconsistencies.

So Genesis, like the other books of the Pentateuch was a mosaic, a patchwork quilt. The Germans printed the Pentateuch by designating each source with a different color. That was how we got the "Rainbow Bible."

Before the printing press, when traditions were handed down orally, it is easy to understand how variations could have arisen in the different traditions. Still, the beautiful unity of Genesis, and Pentateuch as a whole, attests to the fact that when these traditions were written down there had to be a single author orchestrating the writing. That's all divine inspiration means; namely, that God took authors as they were so that each retained his own style; but yet unbeknown to them, God moved each one to write what He, God, wanted to be written. A wonderful unity prevails in the Book of Books, that it can be called by one name "The Bible," having only one author—God!

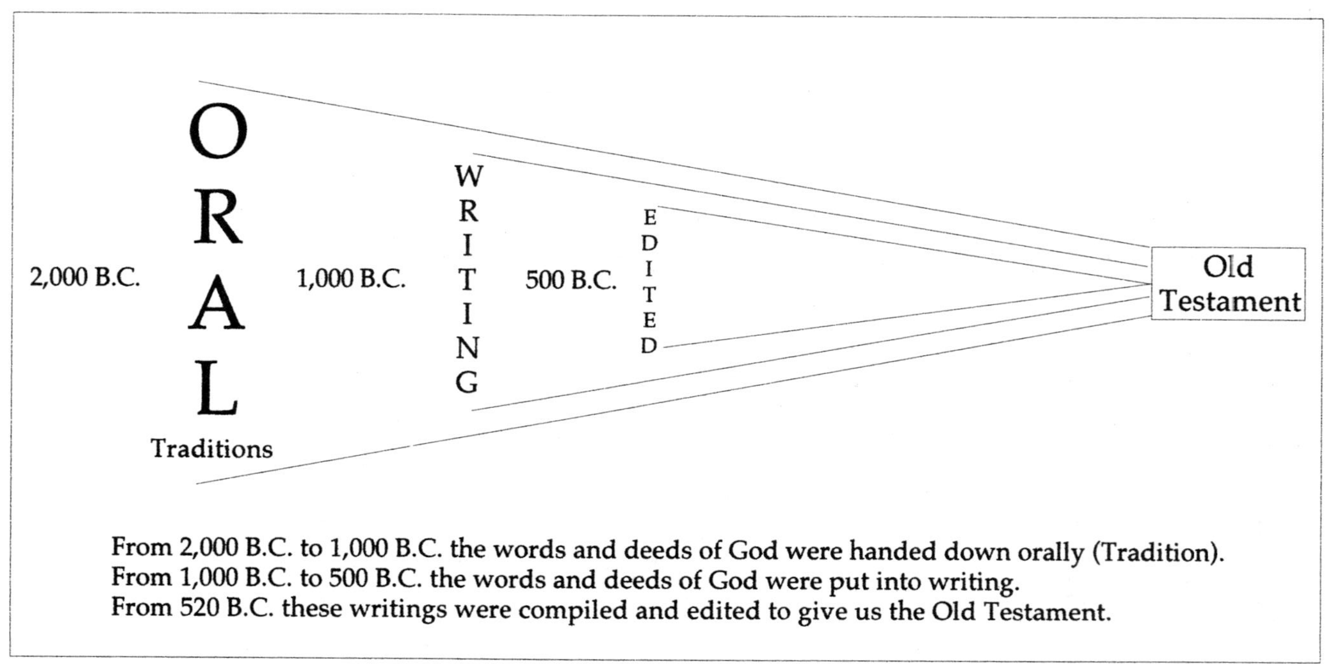

From 2,000 B.C. to 1,000 B.C. the words and deeds of God were handed down orally (Tradition).
From 1,000 B.C. to 500 B.C. the words and deeds of God were put into writing.
From 520 B.C. these writings were compiled and edited to give us the Old Testament.

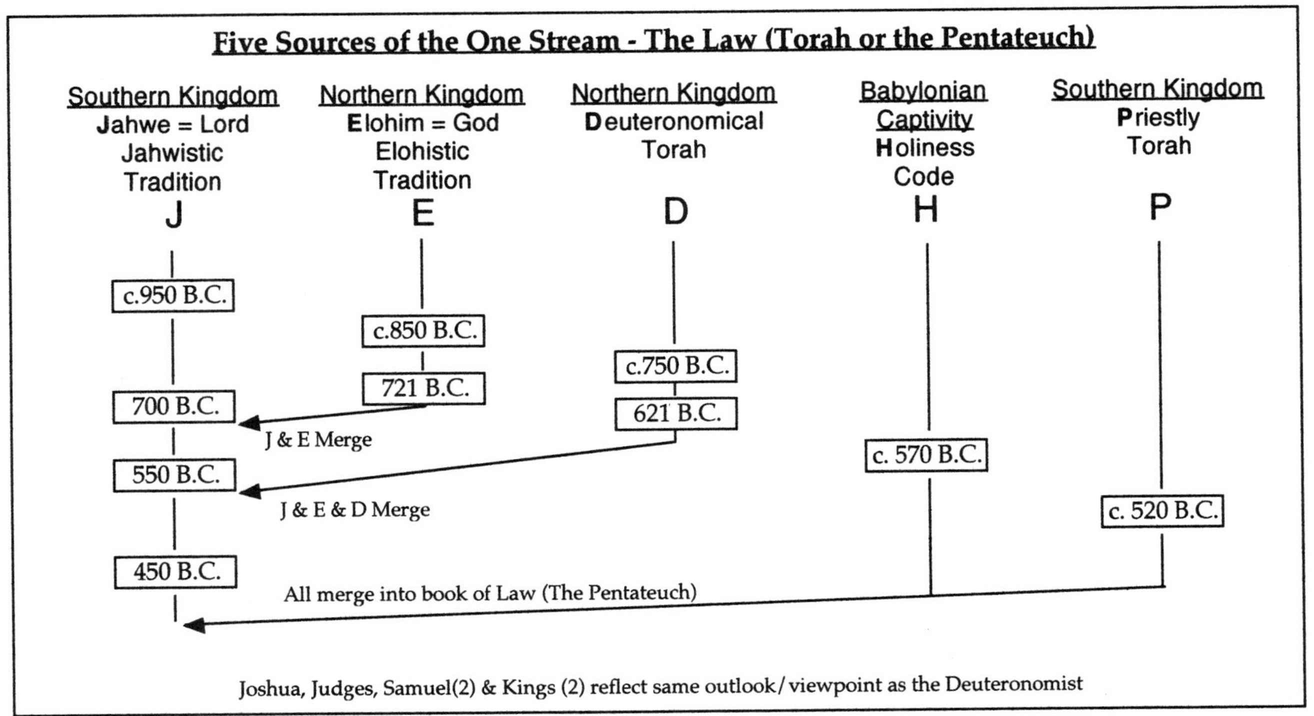

Five Sources of the One Stream - The Law (Torah or the Pentateuch)
Southern Kingdom
Jahwe = Lord
Jahwistic
Tradition
J
Northern Kingdom
Elohim = God
Elohistic
Tradition
E
Northern Kingdom
Deuteronomical
Torah
D
Babylonian Captivity
Holiness
Code
H
Southern Kingdom
Priestly
Torah
P
c.950 B.C.
c.850 B.C.
721 B.C.
c.750 B.C.
621 B.C.
700 B.C.
J & E Merge
550 B.C.
J & E & D Merge
c. 570 B.C.
c. 520 B.C.
450 B.C.
All merge into book of Law (The Pentateuch)
Joshua, Judges, Samuel(2) & Kings (2) reflect same outlook/ viewpoint as the Deuteronomist

Appendix 2

Biblical Timetable

Appendix 2: Biblical Timetable

Stone Age	Paleolithic Age	Mesolithic Age	Neolithic Ice Age	Cities	Writing	Bronze Age	Iron Age
500,000 B.C.?	100,000 B.C.?	15,000 B.C. Adam & Eve (Gn. 1-3) Cain → Abel ↓ ↓ Lamech Seth (Gn.4) Generations Adam to Noah (Gn.5) ↓ Descendants of Lamech & Seth intermarry (Gn.6:1-4) Resulting immorality leads to the Flood Details of Stories (Gn.4-6) are taken from the civilization of 8,000 B.C. We call this Anachronism: details out of date timewise	9,000 B.C. The Flood (Gn. 7-8) Covenant with Noah (Gn.9) Table of the Nations (Gn. 10)	8,000 to 2,000 B.C. ↓ Farming & cattle raising ↓ causes population increase ↓ people united by religion ↓ Shrine marketing city walls ↓ 8,000 B.C. Jericho is built ↓ 6,000 to 2,000 B.C. cities built in Mesopotania ↓ 2,700 B.C. Tower of Babel ↓ 2,600 B.C. Pyramids	3,500 B.C. Sumeria ↓ Cuneiform Writing 4,000 B.C. ↓ 3,100 B.C. in Egypt Hieroglyphics ↓ 2,500 B.C. in Harappa N.W. India	3,000 B.C.	2,500 to 1,200 B.C.

Appendix 2: Biblical Timetable

Line from Shem to Abram
(Gn. 11:10-26)

1830 B.C.	1800 B.C.	1750 B.C.	1700 B.C.	1675 - 1567 B.C.	1650 B.C.	1250 B.C.	1225 - 1175 B.C.
Abram migrates from UR	Abram to Canaan to Egypt 1795 B.C.	Isaac	Jacob	Hyksos In Egypt	Joseph In Egypt	Exodus From Egypt	Conquest of Canaan

See, Carroll, Warren H.
The Founding of Christendom,
Vol 1, pp.14-58

Other Books
By Rev. Albert J. M. Shamon

Our Lady Teaches About Prayer at Medjugorje $1.00

Our Lady Says: Let Holy Mass Be Your Life $1.00

Our Lady Says: Monthly Confession —
    Remedy for the West $1.00

Our Lady Says: Pray the Creed $1.00

Our Lady Teaches About Sacramentals
    and Blessed Objects $1.00

Our Lady Says: Love People $3.00

Three Steps to Sanctity $1.50

The Ten Commandments of God $3.50

Firepower Through Confirmation $5.00

Apocalypse - A Book For Our Times $4.00

The Power of the Rosary $2.00

Behind the Mass $3.50

A Graphic Life of Jesus the Christ $9.00

Preparing for the Third Millennium $2.00

For additional information, contact **THE RIEHLE FOUNDATION**, distributor of Catholic Books.

Please write to: **THE RIEHLE FOUNDATION**
                P.O. Box 7
                Milford OH 45150-0007 USA

THE
RIEHLE
FOUNDATION ...

The Riehle Foundation is a non-profit, tax-exempt, charitable organization that exists to produce and/or distribute Catholic material to anyone, anywhere.

The Foundation is dedicated to the Mother of God and her role in the salvation of mankind. We believe that this role has not diminished in our time, but, on the contrary has become all the more apparent in this the era of Mary as recognized by Pope John Paul II, whom we strongly support.

During the past years the Foundation has distributed books, films, rosaries, bibles, etc. to individuals, parishes, and organizations all over the world. Additionally, the foundation sends materials to missions and parishes in a dozen foreign countries.

Donations forwarded to The Riehle Foundation for the materials distributed provide our sole support. We appreciate your assistance, and request your prayers.

> IN THE SERVICE OF JESUS AND MARY
> All for the honor and glory of God!

The Riehle Foundation
P.O. Box 7
Milford, OH 45150-0007 USA
513-576-0032